W9-AQO-689

Hans-J. Ullmann
with
Evamaria Ullmann

The New Dog Handbook

60 Color Photographs by Outstanding Animal Photographers and 66 Drawings by Günther Marks

Translated from the German by Rita and Robert Kimber
American Advisory Editor Matthew M. Vriends, Ph.D.

CHILDRENS PRESS CHOICE
A Barron's title selected for educational distribution
ISBN 0-516-08682-0

First English language edition published in 1985 by
Barron's Educational Series, Inc.

The title of the German book is *Das neue Hundebuch*

All inquiries should be addressed to:
Barron's Educational Series, Inc.
113 Crossways Park Drive
Woodbury, New York 11797

International Standard Book No. 0-8120-2857-0

Library of Congress No. 84-21577

Library of Congress Cataloging in Publication Data

Ullman, Hans-Jochen.
The new dog handbook.

Translation of: Das neue Hundebuch.
Includes index.
1. Dogs. I. Ullmann, Evamaria. II. Title.
SF427.U6313 1985 636.7 84-21577
ISBN 0-8120-2857-0

Printed in Hong Kong

6 490 987654

Photo Credits

Animal/Thompson: Page 19 middle left, bottom left, bottom right; page 56 middle left, bottom left, bottom right; page 73 middle right, bottom left; page 100 above left, above right, middle left; page 109 bottom right.
Bielfeld: Page 73 bottom right; page 109 bottom left.
Buzzini: Page 37 middle left.
Dossenbach: Page 19 above left; page 127 bottom right
Hinz: Page 37 bottom left; page 56 bottom right; page 73 middle left; page 100 middle right; page 109 middle left; page 127 bottom right; page 128, back cover bottom left, back cover bottom right, back cover middle right.
Interessergemeinschaft deutscher Hundehalter e. V.: Page 19 middle right; page 37 middle right; page 73 bottom left; page 127 middle left, and left.
Dr. Jesse: Page 55.
Roebild: Page 109 above right.
Scheeler/Stern: Back cover middle.
Schneider-Wegler: Front cover; inside front cover; page 9; page 10 bottom, and back cover above right.
Ullmann: Page 19 above right; page 20; page 37 above left, above right, bottom right; page 56 above left, middle right; page 73 above right; page 74; page 99; page 100 bottom left, bottom right; page 109 middle right, bottom left; page 127 above left, middle right, inside back cover, back cover above left.
Vogeler: Page 38; page 110.

About the Authors

Hans-Jochen and Evamaria Ullmann write pet books, and are also dog photographers, and dog owners, with years of experience. During their photo-trips that often lead them to dog shows, they constantly come into contact with dog dealers and dog breeders – and in this way they learn much about the different dog breeds. Their Pet Owner's Manuals "Spaniels" and "Poodles" were published in many countries.

Cover Photos

Front: Wirehaired Dachshund.
Back, above left: Saint Bernard, above right: Young German Shepherd Dog; middle: Mutt; middle right: Siberian Husky; below left: Papillon; below right: Borzoi (Russian Wolfhound).
Inside front cover: Mutt with her puppies.
Inside back cover: Old English Sheepdog – a quiet, intelligent lovable Working Dog, playful and usually boisterous.

Contents

Contents

Contents

Foreword

American scientists have shown that pets have a beneficial effect on their owners' health. People who pet their dogs or cats become calmer, their pulse rate slows down, and high blood pressure drops. However, most of us do not buy our dogs for scientific reasons. We simply want a companion that will adapt itself to us, listen to us, and help us get to know other people. In addition, we have a yearning – especially if we live in big cities – to have a little bit of nature close to us.

Dogs are "a piece of nature." Although bred by humans and adapted to human ways through generations of living with us, they still behave in accordance with the animal instincts of their ancient ancestor, the wolf. If you keep, train, and feed your puppy to suit its dog nature, that is, if you do not pretend it is a human being in fur clothing, you may rest assured that it will grow into a physically fit and psychologically healthy creature.

This *New Dog Book* answers all the major questions that come up in daily life with a dog. You will find out how to recognize physical defects and character weaknesses in your dog; how to raise it so that it will obey your every word and refrain from begging at the table or yapping all the time; how to train it in specific skills, which is important if you plan to show it; how often to bathe it and how to trim its coat and clip its nails; whether to feed it only commercial dog food or raw meat as well; how to get rid of fleas, ticks, and other pests – and much more.

One chapter presents the historical development of dogs and explains their patterns of behavior in detail. You will need this information if you want to educate your dog properly. Another chapter deals with symptoms of illness, infectious diseases, and illnesses typical of certain breeds. It also includes detailed information on first aid and simple treatments, so that you can take care of injuries and minor illnesses yourself. Dr. Isabell Fiebiger of the Veterinary Clinic in Munich (Germany) has gone over this chapter, and I should like to take this opportunity to thank her for her valuable help.

Whether you have just purchased your first puppy or have owned a purebred dog for years, this book can help you find out more about "your kind of dog." A special section of this book presents sixty dog breeds with color photos, drawings, and descriptions. Character traits and specific requirements – for space, exercise, and amount of your time – are discussed here in detail for each breed. I should like to express my gratitude to Mr. Günther Marks for his exceptionally fine drawings and to all the photographers whose excellent pictures contribute so much to the visual attractiveness of this book.

Last but not least I want to thank my wife. Her creativity and loving criticism have helped make this book a truly practical manual you can turn to with all your questions about the care of dogs.

Hans-J. Ullmann

Prerequisites for Keeping a Dog

Love for Animals – What Is It?

The desire to have a dog no doubt arises from a love for animals, but just what is the nature of this love?

Oddly enough, the handling of animals is still bedeviled by opinions and practices that were wrong a hundred years ago but that have been uncritically perpetuated from generation to generation. This is all the more surprising because we pride ourselves on our awareness of environmental issues and our love for nature and for its creatures.

One common view holds, for instance, that you can train a dog only if you beat it, "to break its will." The poor creature treated that way will, predictably, become either neurotic and timid or overly aggressive and dangerous. At the other extreme are lapdogs. They have always been considered luxury items for those who treat them like dolls and spoil and feed them to death. The result is obese little dogs that constantly tremble with fear or yap hysterically. Because dog owners expect the general public to have some tolerance for their pets, I should like to explain briefly to them – and to anyone contemplating getting a dog – what "love for animals" really means.

Loving your dog means

- Acquiring a thorough understanding of its real nature and needs as well as of its capabilities;
- Treating it lovingly but always in keeping with its nature and background;
- Training it in such a way that it can adjust as unproblematically as possible to living with people. The owner must see to it that the dog does not bother, endanger, or harm anyone and that the dog in turn is not exposed to danger or harm.

The wirehaired fox terrier is one of the dogs that need regular walks and plenty to do.

- Taking enough time and having enough patience to give it the exercise it needs, neither overtaxing it nor leaving it to its own devices for extended periods without encouragement or set tasks.
- Performing whatever grooming tasks are necessary and feeding it properly.
- Caring for it lovingly and understandingly, even when it is sick and old.

If you are willing to put these principles into practice, then you are a true animal lover, and a dog will live a happy life with you.

Things to Consider Beforehand

The next step toward realizing your dream of having a four-footed friend is to consider the legal, financial, practical, and personal aspects of owning a dog. Take the time to answer the following questions, even though some of them have already been touched on in our definition of love for animals.

Do I have:

• *Permission from my landlord,* preferably in writing, to keep a pet?

Prerequisites for Keeping a Dog

• *Enough space* to house a dog properly so that it has both a comfortable retreat and ample opportunity to move about?

• *Enough time* for daily activities with my dog, especially for daily walks, education, and grooming, all of which are absolutely necessary and quite time-consuming?

• *Enough energy and consistency* to train my dog?

• *Enough emotional stability and staying power* to assume responsibility for my pet in any and all situations for as long as the animal lives?

• *Sufficient financial means* to cover the costs of keeping a dog throughout its lifetime (food, accessories, veterinarian's bills, dog license, and insurance)?

If you have answered all the questions with an unqualified yes, you pass the test for being a good pet owner.

Wish and Reality

Now is the time to ask yourself what kind of dog you'd like to have. Chances are you'll wish for an intelligent and beautiful animal, one that is not too big and not too small, eager to learn and easy to train, good with children but also a good watchdog, and easy and economical to keep. Of course, no one dog will have all these qualities, which seem so desirable from a human point of view. You therefore must select the qualities that matter most to you and look for breeds that have them.

You are probably familiar with a number of breeds already. Your neighbor may have a dachshund, or your aunt, a poodle. Ask these people about their dogs, and you will get some sense of what it is like to live with a dog.

Sometimes, however, it is the less obvious qualities of a dog that prove annoying. A dog may be the right size and behave well in most respects but have a habit of snoring in its sleep or breathing loudly at the slightest exertion or excitement. You may find this cute in a puppy, but later it may get on your nerves and drive you crazy. Of course, everything depends on how master and dog feel about each other and how long the first infatuation lasts and helps you overlook a minor defect of this kind. Problems like this should never be solved by simply getting rid of a dog that has become used to living with you. A dog that has started to accept a person as its master and to subordinate itself–in the manner of its ancestors–to this "leader of the pack," would suffer inordinately and have a hard time accepting another human. You need to take this and other matters I will discuss later into consideration before making even a careful choice, much less buying the "dog of your dreams" on an impulse.

The Range of Breeds

There are over 300 dog breeds. The largest of these is the Irish wolfhound, which can measure as much as 32 to 36 inches (80 to 90 centimeters) at the withers. At the other end of the scale is the chihuahua, which may stand no more than 6 inches (15 centimeters) tall. Between them is the rest of the clan, varying in height and shape like the pipes of an organ. The breeds also differ in the quality and quantity of their fur. The coat of a Mexican hairless

The Saint Bernard is especially fond of children. It should be kept outdoors and needs daily exercise.

for instance, consists of no more than a tuft of hair on the head and a tassel at the end of the tail, but the komondor, the Hungarian "king of sheepdogs," is covered from head to tail with long, shaggy strands. Between these two extremes there are all imaginable hair lengths, textures, and colors, as well as other differences. Deciding what kind of dog to get is no simple matter.

There are, of course, books that describe the dog breeds, arranging them alphabetically or by origin or primary use, but most people interested in getting a dog do not need a lot of technical information. They are simply animal lovers who want a canine companion. They do not want to travel from dog show to dog show, collecting ribbons and awards, nor do they want to build up a kennel. The basic character traits of a breed interest them more than the anatomical details, ideal measurements, and flawless pedigrees needed to win fame and recognition in the dog world. Prospective owners want to know what it is like to live with a specific kind of dog. Most people who already have, or are about to get, a dog look to a book like this one for advice in practical, everyday matters.

The first question is what kind of dog to get, and this choice is not as difficult as it may at first seem. Of the more than 300 breeds that exist, only about 200 are recognized by the major dog associations. Of these breeds, only about 100 are more or less common, with only

Above: When dogs meet, they always start out by sniffing noses. Shown in this picture are an Afghan hound (left) and a young bearded collie mutt.
Below: Dogs and other domestic animals get along fine if they know each other as well as this wirehaired dachshund and rooster do.

Breeds range from very large to tiny toy dogs. Choose a dog that fits your way of life as well as your living quarters.

about 50 enjoying what could be called popularity. Finally, the breeds recognized as favorites the world over number only about 25.

To help you make your choice, I have included descriptions of the sixty most popular breeds (pages 97–131) that will make it easy for you to figure out which of them suit you, your living arrangements, and your way of life. You can also consult The Most Common Dog Breeds at a Glance (pages 13–15).

In the descriptions of external characteristics, I was able to restrict myself to essentials, since pictures say more than a thousand words. Experts and breeders will want to consult the standards prescribed by their breed's association for desirable physical appearance and character traits. If you are interested in these matters, you can write for guidelines to the American Kennel Club (AKC) or to specific breed associations (Addresses, page 132).

My descriptions in this book focus more on which breeds are suitable for which kinds of people. I tell you what character traits you will find in a typical example of any given breed, and also the breed's most common problems. In addition to color, size, and weight, you will find how much space and exercise a particular dog needs and how much time and effort are involved in grooming and care.

Start by making a preliminary selection. Pick those dogs in the table that come closest to your expectations. The page references indicate where to find a photo of the breed and a description that covers the most important physical qualities and character traits. I am convinced that after weighing this information in the light of your personal circumstances, you will come up with the right choice for you and your family.

Do remember that a dog is only as good as its education. Purebred lineage plays only a secondary role here, and an ordinary mutt may often have better manners than an aristocratic, prize-winning champion with an impressive list of forebears. In the final analysis it will be up to you, and only you, how well your dog will turn out.

The Most Common Dog Breeds at a Glance

	For small homes	For large homes with access to a yard	Suitable for beginners	Gets along well with children	Has qualities of a hunting dog	Can be used as a working dog	Needs extensive grooming	Needs less grooming	Needs a lot of exercise	Needs less exercise	Description on page	Illustration on page
Afghan hound		×			×		×		×		97	10/20
Airedale Terrier		×		×		×		×	×		119	100
Basset hound		×		×				×	×		114	109
Beagle	×		×	×	×			×	×		122	109
Bedlington terrier		×	×	×				×	×		119	119
Bernese mountain dog		×		×		×	×		×		103	37
Borzoi		×			×		×		×		97	BC
Boston terrier	×							×		×	120	
Boxer		×		×		×		×	×		108	56
Bullterrier		×				×		×	×		120	100
Cavalier King Charles spaniel	×		×	×	×		×			×	125	125
Chihuahua	×		×					×		×	125	127
Chow chow		×		×			×			×	115	73
Cocker spaniel, American and English		×	×	×	×		×		×		115	73/74/99/115
Collie		×		×			×		×		103	37
Dachshund – Long-haired	×		×	×	×		×		×		123	
– Miniature, long-haired	×		×	×	×		×			×	123	
– Miniature, short-haired	×		×	×	×			×		×		
– Short-haired	×		×	×	×			×	×		123	
– Toy ("rabbit")	×		×	×	×			×		×	123	
– Wirehaired	×		×	×	×			×	×		123	110/38
Dalmatian		×	×	×				×	×		116	73
Doberman pinscher		×				×		×	×		111	56
English bulldog	×			×				×	×		116	117
English toy spaniel – Blenheim	×		×	×	×		×			×	125	
– King Charles	×		×	×	×		×			×	125	
– Prince Charles	×		×	×	×		×			×	125	
– Ruby	×		×	×	×		×			×	125	

The Most Common Dog Breeds at a Glance

	For small homes	For large homes with access to a yard	Suitable for beginners	Gets along well with children	Has qualities of a hunting dog	Can be used as a working dog	Needs extensive grooming	Needs less grooming	Needs a lot of exercise	Needs less exercise	Description on page	Illustration on page
Fox terrier – Smooth		×		×	×			×	×		120	100
– Wirehaired		×		×	×			×	×		120	7
French bulldog	×		×					×		×	124	109
French mastiff (dogge de bordeaux)		×				×		×		×	97	98
German pointer – Long-haired		×		×	×		×		×		104	
– Short-haired		×		×	×			×	×		104	38
– Wirehaired		×		×	×			×	×		104	
German shepherd		×		×		×		×	×		111	55
German spaniel (wachtelhund)		×			×		×		×		104	104
Golden retriever		×		×	×	×	×		×		105	37
Great Dane		×		×		×		×	×		98	19
Hovawart		×		×		×		×	×		98	19
Irish wolfhound		×		×	×	×		×	×		101	19
Komondor		×						×		×	105	19
Kromfohrländer	×		×	×				×	×		117	73
Kuvasz		×		×		×		×	×		106	106
Lhasa Apso	×		×				×			×	126	127
Maltese	×						×			×	126	127
Mexican hairless (Xoloitzcuintle); also Chinese crested dog and hairless dog (cane nudo; "African")	×							×		×	129	127
Münsterländer – Grosser (large)		×			×				×		106	37
– Kleiner (small)		×			×			×	×		106	
Neapolitan mastiff		×				×		×		×	101	19
Newfoundland		×		×		×	×		×		102	19
Old English sheepdog (bobtail)		×		×		×	×		×		107	IBC
Papillon	×		×				×			×	129	BC
Pekingese	×		×				×			×	129	127
Pinscher	×		×					×		×	130	127

The Most Common Dog Breeds at a Glance

	For small homes	For large homes with access to a yard	Suitable for beginners	Gets along well with children	Has qualities of a hunting dog	Can be used as a working dog	Needs extensive grooming	Needs less grooming	Needs a lot of exercise	Needs less exercise	Description on page	Illustration on page
Pointer		×		×	×			×	×		107	37
Poodle – Miniature	×		×	×			×			×	117	117
– Standard		×		×			×		×		117	73
– Toy	×		×				×			×	117	
Pug	×		×	×				×		×	124	109
Rottweiler		×		×		×		×	×		112	56
Saint Bernard		×		×		×	×			×	102	9/BC
Saluki		×			×			×	×		103	20
Schnauzer – Giant		×		×		×		×	×		112	56
– Miniature	×		×	×				×	×		112	
– Standard	×		×					×	×		112	49
Scottish terrier	×			×			×			×	121	100
Setter – English – Gordon – Irish		×		×	×		×		×		108	37
Shih Tzu	×		×	×			×			×	130	
Siberian husky	×			×				×	×		113	56/BC
Skye terrier		×		×			×			×	121	100
Spitz group – Keeshond		×		×			×			×	114	
– Pomeranian	×		×				×			×	114	
– Wolfsspitz		×		×			×			×	120	56
Stichelhaar (German rough-haired pointer)		×		×	×			×	×			
Welsh corgi – Cardigan	×		×	×				×		×	124	109
– Pembroke			×	×				×		×	124	
West Highland white terrier	×		×	×			×			×	122	
Whippet	×							×	×		118	118
Yorkshire terrier	×		×				×			×	122	100

Considerations Before You Buy

Where and When Should You Buy Your Dog?

Let us assume that you have made your choice or have narrowed it down to two or three breeds. What is the next step? Where can you go to look at dogs and then select and buy one?

The best method is to go to a kennel that specializes in the breed you are interested in. Do not buy your pet from a "dog factory" that engages in mass breeding – usually of many breeds – for purely commercial reasons. Do not let yourself be tempted by the "special offers" of some dealer, and, above all, do not do business with mail-order companies, which are totally profit-oriented. If you do, you may end up with a mentally disturbed or physically impaired animal because many serious defects are not evident to the lay person at first glance. As in all fields of commerce there are unscrupulous dealers, and even some breeders take their responsibilities too lightly and do not hesitate to make money selling sick dogs. It does not seem to concern these people that such practices lend a bad name to the whole profession.

The moral of all this is, keep a sharp eye out when buying a dog! Avoid all risk, and get all pertinent advice ahead of time from the dog club of the breed you have chosen. Such a club will tell you when reputable kennels have puppies for sale. Dealers approved by the central office of a breed association will also help you out with information and arrange for you to get a puppy from a serious breeder.

The best time to get a puppy is when the litter is about eight to ten weeks old. At this point, the puppies are weaned and have learned to eat solid food from a bowl, so that no major feeding problems are likely when they move to their new homes. (Refer to page 58 to find out how to feed a puppy properly.) Younger puppies still need their mothers. If the young dogs are more than ten weeks old and have been continually locked up, they may have trouble getting used to new people and a new place because they are past the imprinting phase (page 93).

What to Watch for When You Buy

- You should make up your mind neither too late nor too early about which puppy you want to buy, and you should allow a little time to get acquainted before you bring it home. This will make the transition from the kennel to the home easier both for the puppy and for you.
- Check first to see if everything is as it should be in the kennel. Examine the quarters and the general health of the puppies and, if possible, of their dam. Are they all healthy, dewormed, and vaccinated? (See diseases, disorders, vaccinations, page 72.)
- Watch the puppy of your choice to see if it is excessively shy and timid. In a puppy six weeks old, these signs might indicate some mental imbalance that will persist for the rest of its life. A healthy young dog is curious and comes running up to anyone who approaches it in a friendly manner.
- If you are buying a dog of recognized breed, ask to see its papers. In this document, called a pedigree, the local chapter and the national office of the breed association officially confirm that the dog in question is a purebred. This gives you at least a minimal guarantee that your dog is descended from excellent stock.

Considerations Before You Buy

You should buy your puppy when it is eight to ten weeks old. At this point it already shows the typical traits of its breed and is beginning to become independent.

Do not buy a dog in a hurry. Take the time to plan and check everything. An animal is not an item of merchandise that you can exchange if you do not like the looks of it later. The purchase is more like an adoption. You are acquiring a living creature that will, if all goes well, grow up happy and healthy in your family and be part of your life for twelve or fifteen years, sometimes even longer.

Don't Buy on Impulse

"Look before you leap!" This warning is as relevant to the purchase of a dog as it is to any other decision, and it is a rare animal lover who is totally immune to making a rash, spur-of-the-moment purchase that may later be regretted. The approach of Christmas, a birthday, or an anniversary may trigger the bright idea that a puppy would be just the thing for a friend or relative. Or, as you pass the window of a pet store, you may see some irresistible puppies that you are tempted to buy, partly out of pity for these animals displayed behind glass. But stop and think. How will a pet you have bought on a whim and given to someone as a present fare later when the recipient's first enthusiasm wears off? How will the dog be housed? Who will look after it and spend time with it? These questions are particularly to the point if the puppy is intended for children. How quickly the fun of looking after a pet can turn into a chore! If there is any possibility that the animal might become a burden or an imposition on personal freedom, you should think twice before giving an animal as a gift and refrain from such a purchase. There are enough homeless creatures in animal shelters already; do not add to their number.

Why Choose a Purebred Dog?

If you want to do a good deed, you can go to an animal shelter and pick out a dog to bring home. There you will find big and little dogs of various breeds (some even with pedigrees), as well as mongrels, many of which are just as intelligent and trainable as purebreds. If your heart is not set on owning a pedigreed dog and you have no interest in champions and prizes, you may be perfectly happy with a nondescript mutt. Choosing a young dog of unknown background is a little like playing roulette, however: you can win or lose. There is no way of telling what kind of dog a young puppy will turn into. It might grow much larger than anticipated, which can create problems. And, you cannot predict in a mongrel what character traits will predominate because usually there is little indication of the various breeds in its background. You inevitably take a risk, but in most cases the gratitude of the animal that was freed from the confinement of a shelter will more than make up for any shortcomings.

One more point: Statistics gathered in West Germany show that the number of people bitten by mongrels is only about half as great as that of people bitten by pedigreed dogs. The main explanation is probably that purebred dogs are more prone to degeneration, particularly when a breed that has caught on is "mass-produced." Another contributing factor may be the excessive concern for external breed characteristics that some breeders have. In some breeds, too, an unnatural physical build is called for in the standard. An example is the excessively long body and relatively short legs of bassets and Skye terriers. Other examples of breeding for effect—and thereby creating defects—are the efforts to achieve excessively large or small sizes in some breeds and the deliberate propagating of mutations, such as the exaggerated skin folds of the Shar Pei and the absence of fur in the Mexican hairless.

Then, too, purebred dogs are sometimes acquired primarily as status symbols and are trained either carelessly or not at all. Mongrels, on the other hand, generally appeal to people who know dogs and are likely to love them and look after them properly.

If you want to have a dog of a particular breed that you want to enter in shows and to train in obedience and special skills, you should look for a purebred. Purebred dogs have certain inherited traits and skills, which are mentioned in the Description of Dog Breeds starting on page 97. Their external appearance is also determined by their parentage, and the expert will always recognize the breed beyond any doubt. This kind of recognition is impossible with mongrels. Purebred dogs should, if at all possible, be allowed to use their special talents. A German shepherd that is eager to work should not live a sedentary indoor life, and a little chihuahua would make a poor watchdog. A keeshond is better than a burglar alarm, but a friendly beagle would greet robbers with a wagging tail. There are also many specialized working dogs among purebreds: watchdogs, stock dogs, guard and rescue dogs, hunting dogs, and dogs for pulling sleds, as well as those that guide the blind or detect narcotics, to mention just a few. My point is that the owner of a purebred dog will know what to expect from a dog, but the owner of an ordinary mutt may be in for some surprises. Be sure, then, you are aware of all the implications of your choice.

Male or Female?

You often hear that female dogs become more attached to their "masters" than to their "mistresses" and that male dogs prefer female humans. Another common prejudice is that male dogs are easier to keep than females but that the latter are more affectionate and loyal. Neither of these claims is true, and there are lots of cases that disprove them. (Our male cocker spaniel, for instance, is just as attached to me as to my wife.) How should you decide what to get, then? Leni Fiedelmeier, a well-known writer on dogs, offers the following tip:

"Before you make your decision, have a look around your neighborhood. Are more male dogs being taken out for walks than females? If so, then decide in favor of a male. If females predominate, however, get a female.

Large dogs.
Above left: brindled Great Dane; above right: Irish wolfhounds.
Center left: Newfoundland; center right: komondor (Hungarian herdsman's dog).
Below left: Neapolitan mastiff; below right: Hovawart.

The reason? If you keep a male dog on a block where most of the dogs are females, you are likely to have some trouble with him."

This makes sense because a healthy male dog cannot resist the scent of a bitch in heat (page 39) and will use any opportunity to get away and approach her. A bitch is in heat twice annually for a few days and will be just as unreliable and disobedient at these times as an amorous stud.

The only thing you can do as a preventive measure is to give your bitch chlorophyll tablets during these critical days. These pills inhibit the production of the female scent. Repeated injections of estrus-suppressive hormones are not recommended because, in the long run, they may cause hormonal imbalances and related health problems.

Another way to avoid the problems associated with heat is to have your bitch spayed. In this operation, which is called a panhysterectomy, the ovaries and the uterus are removed. You should have your dog spayed only if you are absolutely sure that you will not want puppies.

If you have a male dog, you have to be more patient when you take him for walks. He will want time and opportunity to sniff and to mark his territory by leaving his scent. You will also have to display some understanding for his restlessness if he senses the presence of a bitch in heat nearby or even quite far away. At these times you should show your neighbors and any owners of female dogs the courtesy of always keeping your dog on a leash and under control.

Greyhounds need a lot of movement, especially running free.
Above: Afghan hounds; below: Salukis.

Whether you choose a male or a female dog is purely a matter of personal preference; both require patience and understanding.

A healthy male dog marks his territory by leaving little squirts of urine behind. You therefore should be more patient when taking a male dog for a walk than when taking out a female.

Puppy or Grown Dog?

This decision, too, is completely up to you. It can be extremely satisfying to see a puppy grow up from clumsy babyhood into a well-behaved companion who "understands" practically everything. There is no doubt that an association that starts this early in the dog's life results in an especially happy relationship between dog and master. Rearing a puppy, though, requires a lot of patience, effort, and time because all the things that seem so natural and easy in the grown dog must be painstakingly taught. And that is no small task, as Training Your Dog (page 44) shows.

Compassion is probably the main argument for choosing a grown dog. There are all too many homeless dogs in animal shelters, waiting for loving humans to offer them new homes. Anyone who adopts one of these poor creatures and provides it with a life worth living deserves praise and proves that he or she is a true animal lover, and a dog released from loneliness this way will usually be particularly loyal and affectionate.

You should be aware that not only the physical but also the psychic development of a grown dog is complete. You may not be able to influence its behavior much, and it is also possible that the animal will not be able to forget its former master and adopt you instead. There are, however, many examples where such second bonds have worked out very well.

To summarize, I would say, if you want to raise and train a young dog, you must be prepared to put in a lot of effort. If you are thinking of getting a grown dog, on the other hand, you will need more sensitivity and understanding. Make your own decision on the basis of this information.

Housing and Equipment

To make sure the new member of your household will be comfortable, you will have to make a few preparations before its arrival. You will find all the equipment you need at this stage at a good pet shop. Don't be overwhelmed by the sheer mass of accessories and luxury articles you find there. Entrepreneurs are well aware that there are many affluent dog owners, and the market therefore offers not only the items necessary for basic care but also many articles you can perfectly well do without.

To help you remember everything you do need, I have made up the following list.

Necessary Equipment

Harnesses for dogs are available in different sizes. Some are without a breast strap (above left) and some with (above right), and in some the leather is sewn into a round shape rather than a flat strap (below).

- A *lined leather collar* is ideal for a dog with a short neck. For dogs that absolutely refuse to wear a collar (chows and Pomeranians are in this category), a *harness* is better.
- A *dog leash* (normal length) is used for walks. For very large dogs, a leather leash with some chain at the end (and perhaps a chain collar) may work better, but chain leashes should not be used with young dogs that still like to chew on everything.
- A *long leash* (one with a spring that automat ically takes up the leash is most practical) can be used for longer walks as well as for training a young dog.
- A *muzzle* may come in handy with snappy bitches during copulation, on trips, and possibly for visits to the veterinarian.
- A *sleeping basket* has to be long enough for the *grown* dog to stretch out in it comfortably. Small dogs often like covered sleeping

Leather (above) and chain (below) choke collars tighten when the dog pulls on the leash. Those made of leather come without a stop ring (above left) and with one (above right). Chain choke collars that tighten only to a certain point (below left) are used for large dogs, and the ones with spurs (below right) are meant for training.

baskets, but those without a top are easier to keep clean.

- A *pad* (one with a washable cover that unzips is most practical) should be warm but not too soft. An old blanket will do fine, but make sure whatever you use is washable.
- You need two *food dishes* because the dog should always have water available. Plastic dishes are not as good as the somewhat heavier (and also more expensive) glazed

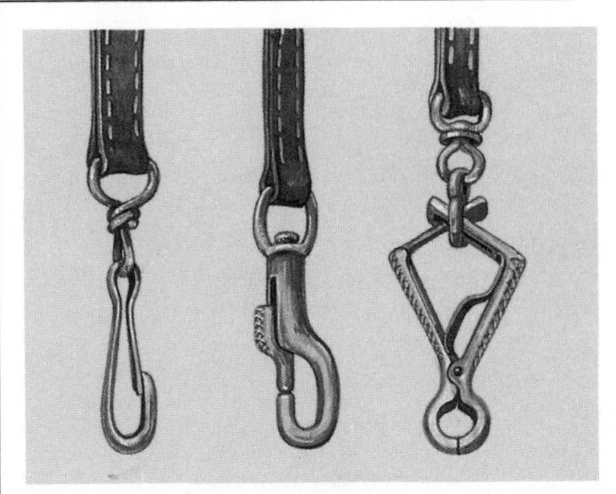

Spring clips for dog leashes: a simple spring clip (left), a clip with a safety catch (center), and a scissor-type clip (right).

Here are several types of food dishes: a plain one made of heavy material (above left), one with a narrow opening for dogs with lop ears (above right), one with a stand for large dogs (center), and a food and water dish on a stand (below).

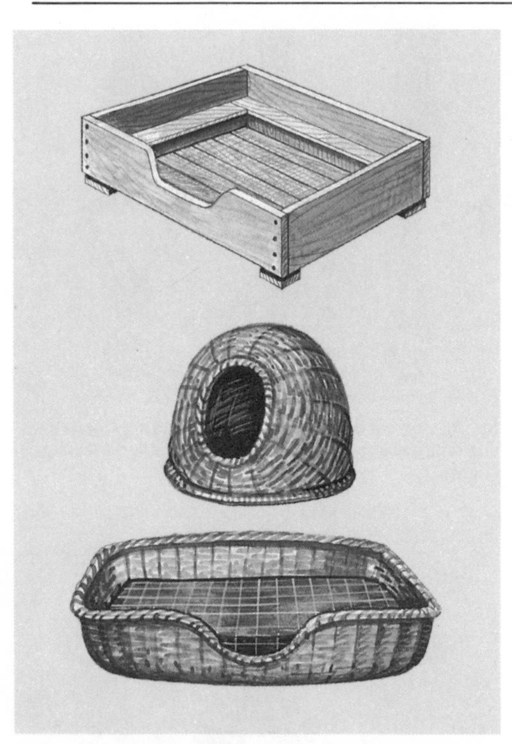

A sleeping box (above) that can also be used as a whelping box; a cavelike covered basket (center) that is popular with smaller dogs; and a regular sleeping basket (below). Make sure that the box or basket you buy is large enough so that the fully grown dog will still fit in it.

stoneware or earthenware. If equipped with rubber strips on the bottom, these heavy dishes cannot be pushed around even by large dogs. For dogs with lop ears there are special food dishes that narrow toward the top so that cocker spaniels or poodles will not spatter their freshly combed ears at every meal. Another practical invention is a little rack that keeps both dishes in place.

- *Metal comb and brush.* The dealer at the pet

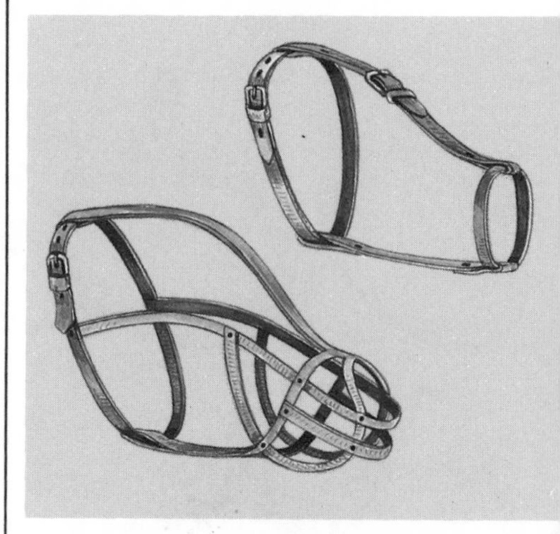

Two types of muzzles: a simple leather loop (above), and a sturdier model with more straps (below).

store will recommend the grooming tools best suited for your dog. You will need a *narrow-toothed "louse comb,"* because even with the best of care dogs occasionally have fleas. For many breeds you will need a wide-toothed comb as well.

Brushes with natural bristles are used on short-haired dogs; rough-haired or long-haired breeds are groomed with a wire brush (or a currycomb). For dogs with very thin, short hair, a grooming glove is practical. The length of the teeth on the comb and the bristles on the brush should be in keeping with the length of the dog's fur. For breeds that should be clipped periodically (poodles, for example), you will need electric clippers with two heads if you plan to clip your dog yourself rather than take it to a dog-grooming parlor. You will not need the clippers until the dog is fully grown. For breeds that need to be trimmed, such as terriers, you can use various stripping tools. Easy to use are stripping combs with serrated teeth and tools with a sharp, smooth, razorlike blade.

- *Tweezers and flea powder* to get rid of ticks and other parasites.
- A *solid rubber ball* for playing and a *rawhide bone* for chewing (the bone helps clean and strengthen the teeth).
- It is also a good idea to have two or three cans of *dog food* or some dry dog food as well as some *dog biscuits* on hand when the dog arrives so that you will not be tempted during the first few days to still its hunger with table scraps.

These are the basic necessities. In addition, I would recommend a few other practical items.

- A *spray foam* that serves as a waterless bath and protects against fleas and other pests, or a *dry shampoo* that serves the same function and is especially useful for puppies, which should not be bathed.
- A *spray* that restores the natural gloss to the dog's coat. This spray deodorizes and protects the fur and should be applied after every grooming session and especially in damp weather.
- *Ear swabs* for the regular care of the dog's ears, especially for lop-eared breeds.
- A *protective spray for the paws* to be used primarily before winter walks on ice and snow. This spray protects against road salt and keeps the pads from getting sore and cracked.
- A *flea collar* offers good protection against fleas, lice, and ticks for two to four months.
- *Disinfectants* to destroy pathogens. Disinfectants can be used on the dog and its bed, the doghouse, and the run.
- *Repellent spray.* This covers up the smell of urine and protects house corners, entryways, furniture, carpet, trees, and shrubs, against further abuse.
- *Scent-inhibiting tablets and sprays* diminish the scent a bitch in heat produces.
- *Protective panties* that come in different sizes (small, medium, and large) and that are made of tough, waterproof material keep a bitch in heat from leaving stains all over the apartment.
- *Rubber massage brushes* or *rubber grooming gloves* are useful for the coat care of short-haired breeds.
- A recent innovation, *leather leashes* and *collars with light-reflective foil* that show up whenever light hits them and help drivers see your dog at dusk and in the dark, protect you and your dog on evening walks on the road.
- A *small leather pocket* attached to the collar and containing your address and some coins so that a finder can call you if your dog has run away, or a metal *address tag*.
- *Dog sweaters* keep cold-sensitive dogs warm in the winter.

Watch Out When Buying Dog Toys

Toys are not a superfluous luxury for dogs. Puppies need to strengthen their teeth and exercise their chewing muscles. Even grown dogs need chewing toys to help keep their teeth clean and prevent calculus from forming. It is essential that these toys be made of a substance that is harmless and suitable for dogs.

Squeaky toys that are sold at pet stores are inappropriate for two reasons. They are made of a kind of plastic that can easily be chewed to bits, and they contain a dangerous metal object, the squeaker. The dog might swallow the squeaker or some of the plastic, and surgery could be required to remove it. Not only synthetic materials – including the cellophane or plastic casings on cheese and sausages – represent a danger, but also all objects made of splintery or easily chewable wood.

The best toys for dogs are balls made of solid rubber (which cannot be chewed to pieces) and chewing toys made of rawhide. Your dog can work on them as long as it likes without the slightest danger. Another side benefit is that your puppy will be occupied by them and less likely to try its sharp little teeth on your furniture.

License Fees, Liability, and Health Insurance

In most countries dogs must be licensed and should be insured. Whether justly or unjustly, dogs are the only domestic animal subject to a license fee, although they are not usually required to be licensed until they are six months old. Many countries, however, grant exemptions to dogs employed in selected occupations. The terms, costs, and conditions of the licenses in the United States vary widely.

So, whether you like it or not, you must pay a license fee for any dog. In exchange for a license fee, you receive a dog tag that the animal must wear whenever it is outside your home or off your property. Dogs found without a valid tag can be taken to the pound. If you see a dog (or wild animal) with signs of rabies in areas where there is danger of rabies or where deer range, it is advisable to phone an animal control agency or the police. The typical rabid dog is in a staggering, glazed-eyed, aggressive condition.

I would also urge you to take out liability insurance on your dog because, as its owner, you are responsible for any damage it causes, whether you are personally at fault or not. The law says that if an animal harms a person either physically or mentally or causes damage to property, the owner of the animal is obliged to compensate the injured party.

If you keep in mind how easily a roaming dog can cause a traffic accident, the annual premium for liability insurance is a small price to pay for peace of mind, on the financial front at least. The only dogs to which the principle of compensation for damages does not apply are specialized "working dogs," such as police, guard, and forest service dogs and, under certain conditions, Seeing Eye dogs, if there is sufficient evidence that a dog belongs in that category.

It is also possible now to get health insurance for dogs, as well as for cats, birds, fish, and other pets. It is advisable, before buying health and surgical policies, to thoroughly investigate such insurance companies with local (or national) insurance boards.

You can also purchase a life insurance policy for your dog, but such an insurance is difficult to obtain and the cost is extremely high (normally 13 percent or more per year of the total valuation placed upon the dog). Hence, if you have a valuable pet you would like to insure, you should ask your insurance agent for details.

Basic Rules for Keeping and Caring for a Dog

Keeping a Dog Outdoors

Not all dogs feel comfortable in centrally heated "human dens" for any length of time. This is particularly true of thick-haired breeds and large working dogs, such as sled dogs. If a dog is going to live outdoors, it must be physically conditioned to the weather and introduced gradually to its run and to outdoor life. A doghouse should be available for protection against dampness, cold, and heat, but a doghouse will keep it warm only if it is the right size for the dog. If the space inside is too small, the dog cannot move or stretch out properly; if it is too large, the body warmth the dog generates will not be sufficient to keep it warm. To prevent the excess loss of heat, the opening of the doghouse should be just large enough for the dog to pass through unhampered.

The measurements of shipping crates for dogs as suggested by humane societies, listed in the following table, can serve as guidelines for the inner dimensions a doghouse should have. Before actually building a run (or doghouse) for your dog, however, it is a good idea to get advice from an appropriate breed club.

German law requires that a pen for a medium-sized dog weighing over 45 pounds (20 kilograms) have a minimum area of 7 square yards (6 square meters), not counting the shelter. Any humane dog owner will realize that such a confined "prison" is much too small to serve as the dog's turf or territory, which is what it represents, after all.

It is advisable that the run include no materials harmful to the dog's health and be so constructed that the dog cannot injure itself on it. The fence must be high and sturdy enough to prevent the dog's escape. At least one side of the run must be open for the dog to look out. If the ground of the run is not covered with an insulating material, there should be an insulated resting area outside the shelter. The ground of the run should allow liquids to filter through or run off, and the whole area of the run must be kept clean, dry, and free of parasites.

Shoulder height, inches (centimeters)	Breed (example)	Inside dimensions of shipping crates, inches (centimeters)		
		Length	Width	Height
14–18 (35–45)	Bullterrier	30 (75)	20 (50)	22 (55)
18–24 (46–60)	Chow chow WolfsSpitz	38 (95)	24 (60)	28 (70)
24–32 (61–80)	German shepherd, Rottweiler, Hovawart, Doberman	52 (130)	30 (75)	38 (95)
Over 32 (80)	Saint Bernard, Great Dane, Irish wolfhound	64 (160)	34 (85)	46 (115)

For periods of hot weather and bright sunshine, the dog must have a shaded area in addition to the shelter.

Dogs may not be tied in their run.

Adult dogs of the same sex that have had no previous contact with each other may be brought together in the same run only under supervision.

These guidelines should also be considered when building an indoor kennel. Such a kennel should get plenty of daylight. The opening through which light enters should measure at least one-eighth the floor area, and the kennel should have adequate ventilation.

It goes without saying that dogs that are delicate, very small, or with inadequate coats must not be kept outdoors. The same goes for dogs that have lived indoors for several years. The resistance of such animals, even if they have thick fur with a warm undercoat, is not comparable to that of wild animals. As domesticated creatures they depend on humans to protect them against the harsh elements.

Sleeping and Feeding Areas

Routine is half of life. Just as we are used to the patterns and regularity of our day, dogs have a desire for a fixed daily routine. They have something like an internal clock that tells them accurately when things are supposed to happen. This internal sense of time together with an innate aversion to change makes our dogs into creatures of habit with a clear sense of order.

It is therefore important—and in your interests as well—to find a spot in your home that will be your dog's future sleeping and resting place. Choose a quiet and draft-free corner where the dog will not be disturbed and where it will be comfortable. As a member of the household, it should not be cut off from family and all the goings-on of family life.

There should also be a set place for feeding. The kitchen or bathroom is the best location because the floor there is usually easily washable, and it is no tragedy if some food is spilled.

When you have made all these preparations, you are ready for the arrival of the new member of the household.

Helping Your Dog Get Settled

If you are going to pick up your dog from a kennel by car, it is useful to take another person along who can hold the puppy on his or her lap and pet it. This diminishes the trauma of being separated from the kennel mates. The body contact and the friendly treatment have a calming effect and help the puppy get adjusted to new people without panicking.

With the first sniffing of your home, a new life starts for your puppy. It needs your help to make this adjustment. Show the puppy its bed, and give it time to examine everything in peace. Lift it gently into its basket, and soothe it by talking sofly and petting it. The puppy will soon understand that this is its own place, its refuge, its bed.

The confidence it will have gained and its curiosity will soon spur it on to inspect its new world more closely and to sniff it all over. The discovery of your best upholstered chair or of your deliciously soft bed may lead to the first clash between you and your dog. Dogs are great lovers of creature comfort and have an amazing nose for the most luxurious pieces of furniture in a home. If you do not step in energetically at this point, you will, by giving in on the principle of one bed and one bed only, have broken the first cardinal rule of dog training, which is, *be consistent.*

Do not let yourself be carried away by the sight of your "cute" little puppy sleeping peacefully and angelically on the soft covers of your bed. If you do not have the heart to chase your little angel off the bed now, you will never be able to get it off armchairs, pillows, couches, or beds later on. It will keep trying to take over these delightful spots, and it will even have some justification for doing so because you once allowed it in the past. Here, as in all your future efforts at dog training, you must never forget this one rule: *Consistency is the key to harmonious coexistence between dogs and humans!*

If you intend to keep your dog in a pen later on (if it is of a hardy breed suited to outdoor life), you should soon acquaint it with its future living quarters. Take it with you to the pen, show it around, and let it sniff and examine everything. Repeat these visits daily, and gradually increase the time spent there, playing with it a little, feeding it, or letting it take a nap. The young dog will become so used to the pen that you will soon be able to leave it there alone for an hour or two and later for longer periods. While it is not yet fully grown, however, it should still always spend the night indoors. It also belongs inside during very cold weather or when it is sick. It must always feel it is part of the family, even later when it is grown up and "lives" in the pen. This means that you must spend plenty of time with an outdoor dog, taking it for walks and letting it participate in family activities, even when it is fully grown.

The First Few Nights

You must remain firm at night, too. It is imperative that the puppy get used to sleeping in its bed. If for no other than hygienic reasons, dogs have no business sleeping in people's beds. If contact with household pets is too close, there is a danger of zoonosis, that is, the communication of disease from animal to human. The dog belongs in its bed at night, but how do you keep it there if it begins its first night with loud protests and pitiable whines?

Do not lose your nerve. Grit your teeth, and let it howl. If it carries on so vociferously that you worry about your neighbors' sleep, get up briefly and tell it firmly to get into its bed. Calm it and pet it, but do not stay too long, and above all, do not pick it up. It might like that so much that it will resume howling louder than ever when you put it down. During the very first few nights, a rubber hot-water bottle placed under a blanket inside the bed may prove useful. It serves as a substitute for the mother's warmth and usually helps the puppy to go to sleep. These methods of teaching a puppy to stay by itself at night may sound cold and heartless, but they do usually lead to quick success. It is good for the puppy to get used to short periods of being alone. Both the puppy and you will be grateful for this early training later on when it will occasionally have to guard the house by itself for a few hours. By persisting at this early stage, you kill two birds with one stone and score a triumph in your educational efforts that your neighbors (whom you will have informed about the dog's arrival for the sake of good relations) will surely appreciate.

What the Puppy Must Learn Next

The next educational hurdles your puppy must clear are *housebreaking* and *walking on a leash.* Since these projects require not only patience of infinite magnitude but also all your educational talents, they are discussed in detail in Training Your Dog (page 44).

General Grooming

The Coat

Every dog should be groomed thoroughly and regularly, not only for appearance's sake but

Daily grooming is important for all dogs, even for short-haired breeds. Remove all burrs, twigs, and other foreign objects from the fur, and check your dog regularly for ticks and other pests.

also for hygienic reasons and to make it feel good. This applies, too, to short-haired dogs and to all breeds that are neither trimmed nor clipped. The time and effort required for grooming vary with the consistency of the fur. A smooth-haired boxer obviously requires less care than a poodle that must be painstakingly brushed and combed. The cost of having your dog groomed professionally will affect your decision about how much time and effort you invest yourself. Not every dog owner feels comfortable about trimming and grooming, let alone clipping, a dog. Trimming and clipping are essential for only a few breeds, but all dogs need some daily care.

- First, feel your dog all over for any foreign objects and remove them carefully. Burrs, twigs, seed husks of all sorts, and even pieces of wire can get stuck in the fur. If there are ticks to be removed, consult Ticks and Other Pests (page 33).
- For a short-haired dog, you should use a narrow-toothed comb and then a brush with natural bristles. After a thorough combing (*with* the lay of the fur), the dog should be brushed just as thoroughly. To get rid of the last dust and fine hair, you can rub the dog all over with a moist chamois cloth until the coat resumes its natural sheen.
  Rough- and long-haired dogs are first brushed with a wire brush. Brush (without pulling) first with the lay of the fur and then against it until the fur is smooth and pliable.

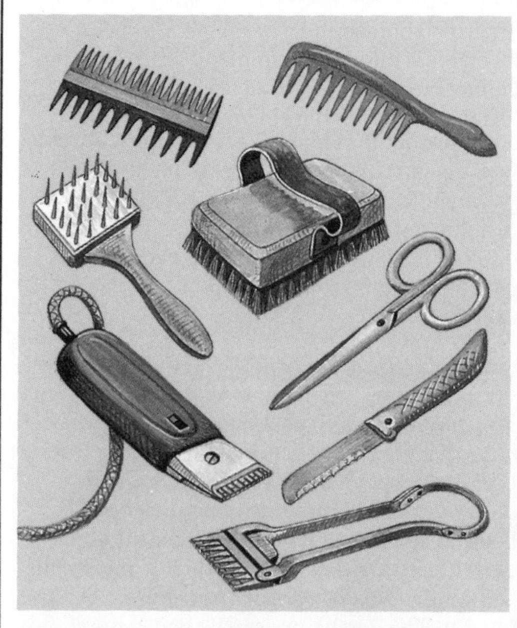

Utensils for grooming: coarse and narrow-toothed combs, wire currycomb, and brush with firm bristles (above). For trimming and clipping: scissors, a trim knife, and hand and electric clippers (below).

Then run a wide-toothed comb, followed by a narrow-toothed comb, over the dog (with the lay of the fur), starting at the head, proceeding down the back to the base of the tail, then down the sides and the legs, and ending with the ears and the tail.

- With some breeds, notably spaniels, this combing and brushing does not altogether do the trick. They must be "plucked" occasionally; that is, the dead hairs must be carefully pulled out between thumb and forefinger. If this is not done, the fur begins to look dull, and the dog begins to itch. The trimming, clipping, and styling that are necessary for some breeds is best left up to a professional in a dog parlor, to begin with, at least. Poodles should be taken there every four to fix weeks, fox terriers, every eight to ten weeks, and Scottish terriers, every six months or so. If someone in your dog club or anyone else with the necessary expertise can teach you, and if you have the time and inclination, you can learn to perform this not altogether easy task yourself. You can get guidelines for standard clips from the dog club of your dog's breed (Addresses, page 132).
- Puppies should get accustomed to these grooming procedures early, but they should be treated very gently so that they will not object to them later.

Bathing

Civilized humans take frequent baths for granted, but the same is not true of dogs, whose skin and hair are impregnated with a natural fatty substance that protects them against adverse weather conditions. Young puppies are not bathed at all; young dogs four months old or more, only when absolutely necessary; and adult dogs, preferably no more than twice a year.

If a dog is dirty, as after a walk in the rain, the only cleaning necessary is to stand it in a plastic tub and rinse its legs and belly off with lukewarm water (without soap). What is important is to rub it down with a towel or use a hair dryer until it is completely dry, so that it will not catch cold or, possibly, get pneumonia.

Dogs have a need to smell "doggy." That is why they like to roll in places that humans consider most offensive. In such a case, of course, a bath is in order. The water should be about 95°F (35°C). Use a foam shampoo especially designed for dogs (available at pet shops), and do not forget to dry your dog completely afterward. Dry shampoos are also available.

Frequent baths are not good for grown dogs, and they also make the hair softer and therefore less resistant to dirt. If you are unlucky, your freshly bathed pet will make straight for the next manure pile to replace the chemical fragrance with something more to its canine liking. Needless to say, it will have to be bathed again, and you can only hope that its offended nose will eventually make its peace with human standards. Long-suffering show dogs pay for their beauty by spending much more time in the bathtub than is good for their health.

Let me emphasize once more: A dog that is brushed and combed regularly should be bathed only if it is really filthy.

Care of Pads and Toenails

Do not neglect to check your dog's feet regularly, for no other part of its body is subject to such hard and constant use as its pads and nails. Pebbles, splinters, thorns, clumps of ice, and other objects can become lodged there and cause pain. The salt used on roads in the winter is especially hard on the pads. That is why you should trim the hair between the toes of long-haired dogs, but do not cut this hair too short because it serves a protective function.

Sore pads should be powdered and cracks treated with Vaseline. In the winter, Vaseline should be rubbed into the paws before a walk, and after the walk they should be washed in lukewarm water and dried. Then, apply baby powder or Vaseline again. If there is a bad cut or the suspicion of a chemical burn, take the dog to the veterinarian.

The nails of dogs that do not get out enough or have too little exercise on rough ground often grow too long. They get caught everywhere and can split. That is why they should be cut periodically. Experienced dog fanciers use nail shears or a coarse nail file for this purpose. A novice dog owner should leave this job up to an expert (at a dog parlor) because blood vessels and sensitive nerve endings are hard to see in dark-colored claws, and you can inflict real damage if you do not know what you are doing.

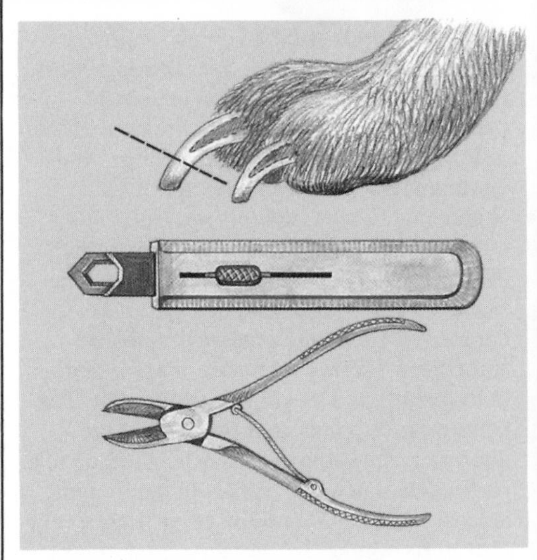
Only an experienced dog owner should attempt to cut the dog's toenails. Nerve endings and blood vessels (above) must not be injured. A claw clipper (center) and claw scissors (below) are the proper instruments to use.

Checking Eyes and Ears

Sometimes small plugs of discharge form in the corners of the eyes, particularly after sleeping, and these should be removed carefully with a clean, lint-free cloth. If there is any inflammation, reddening, tearing, continued blinking, or excessive light sensitivity, the veterinarian should be consulted.

Regular checking of the ears is as important as the care of the eyes. Lop ears and ears with dense hair growth inside them require special

Regular checking and cleaning of the ears is very important, especially for dogs with lop ears or dogs with a lot of hair inside the ears.

attention. At least once a month, dirt, dust, and ear wax should be removed from the ears with a swab dipped in baby oil. Proceed gently, and do not probe too deeply, because the delicate mechanism of the ear can easily be hurt. Check the ear flaps, too, because parasites sometimes lodge there. Remove foreign bodies with fine tweezers. If there is too much hair that sticks together, blocks the entry of the ear, and could lead to obstruction or inflammation, it should be trimmed with round-tipped scissors. In the case of the poodle, hair even grows inside the ear canal itself. Experts pluck these hairs, but this causes the dog pain even if it is done very carefully.

If your dog scratches behind the ears a lot, and/or keeps shaking its head violently, or both, it may be suffering from an inflammation caused by ear mites, the so-called canker of the ear. This condition should be treated by a veterinarian.

Care of Teeth

The teeth of a dog fed a proper diet are self-cleaning. Crunchy food, such as bread crusts, dog biscuits, veal bones, and rawhide bones (page 26) help in this process. Improperly nourished dogs fed food that is deficient in calcium or that is too soft, let alone spicy or sweet, often suffer from calculus, periodontal disorders, and caries, all of which can lead to the loss of teeth.

You can prevent the formation of calculus by cleaning your dog's teeth twice a week with a swab of cotton dunked in lemon juice or a 3% hydrogen solution. Older, hardened deposits should be removed by the veterinarian, because if this is done inexpertly, injuries, inflamed gums, or even infected roots can result.

Ticks and Other Pests

Even the most meticulously cared-for dog may occasionally get fleas or some other parasite. Thanks to modern flea powders, dips, and sprays, it is easy to get rid of these pests. Massage the powder well into the fur and down to the skin. After letting it work for the period indicated in the instructions for use, brush it out thoroughly. The fur must be completely dry for such treatments so that there will be no irritation to the skin.

Ticks, which are a great nuisance for dogs, are harder to deal with. They should be swabbed with alcohol, oil, or a special tick solution (available at pet stores) and then, after about ten minutes, pulled out of the skin with tweezers or special tick pliers (available at pet stores). You must be careful to remove the blood-sucking parasite completely, including the head and the biting parts; otherwise, sores are likely to develop.

If you conscientiously follow the suggestions for care given here and have your pet checked once a year by the veterinarian, you have done everything within your power to prevent diseases and other disorders.

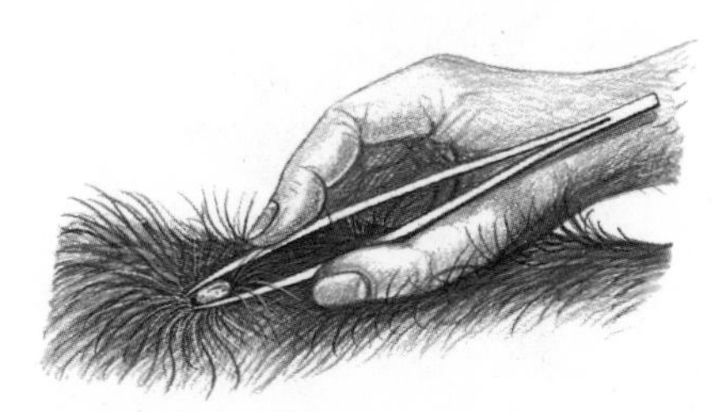

This is how you remove a tick: Dab it with alcohol, oil, or a special tick solution, wait about ten minutes, and then pull it out slowly and carefully with tweezers.

Handling and Play

Picking Your Dog Up—The Right Way

Even people who claim they know everything there is to know about dogs can be observed picking up puppies and sometimes older dogs by grabbing them by the scruff of the neck with one hand. This supposedly expert way of handling dogs is, however, wrong and cruel. Lifting a dog up by its forelegs alone is even more painful for the dog and likely to cause injuries.

If you want to pick up your puppy without hurting it, you place one hand around its chest and support its behind with the other (see drawing, below).

The Importance of Play

Dogs were originally roaming predators, and their hunting instinct is still intact. To stay healthy, they need regular exercise. A dog's body, joints, muscles, and legs are designed for a vigorous outdoor life. Ordinary walks are not challenging enough; they are no substitute for the kind of rigorous exercise that toughens even those muscles that ordinarily get little use. Since our household pets, particularly in the city, have little chance to satisfy their need for movement, let alone their passion for hunting, we must offer them the alternative of play. It is essential that you reserve some time for this every day. Play can easily be combined with a walk because almost all dogs enjoy running after objects and retrieving them.

Everybody, including children, should learn how to lift up a puppy. Place one hand against the rib cage, and support the puppy's rear end with the other.

If you hide or throw a ball, your dog will search for it or run after it with great enthusiasm and bring it back proudly. You can arrange things in such a way that there are obstacles in the dog's path, such as hills or fallen trees it has to clear, or you can hide. Try anything your imagination can come up with. Play exercises not only your dog's body but also its memory and is an excellent aid in dog training.

Your dog should also have a toy to keep it occupied indoors. You will find a great selection of these in pet stores, but check the material carefully. Hollow rubber, celluloid, plastic,and all other synthetic materials are dangerous for pets. Refer once again to Watch Out When Buying Dog Toys (page 25).

Dogs and Children

Almost all dogs are naturally well disposed toward children, but this in itself does not mean much. There are individual differences and occasional exceptions to the rule. Some breeds are especially good with children (see table, page 13, and individual descriptions, page 97) and others are more reserved, indifferent, or positively unfriendly toward childen. And then there are, unfortunately, some dogs that have become neurotic because of genetic defects, poor training, or improper living conditions and are therefore unpredictable and sometimes dangerous. Even a normal dog will, after enough bad experiences with children, learn to distrust them. It is therefore important for parents to teach their children early how to treat a dog properly. Here are the basic topics that should be covered.

- Contrary to many stories and television shows, to which children are constantly exposed, such as the unfortunate *Lassie* series, dogs do not think and act rationally in human terms. You should never expect human actions or reactions from a dog, and you must learn to treat it as what it is, a dog, and let it live in accordance with its inborn needs.
- Never go up to a strange dog and touch it. Wait until it chooses to come up to you with its tail wagging. Do not make any abrupt movements. Let it first sniff the back of your hand, which you carefully reach out toward it, and pet it only if it still acts friendly.
- Treat your own dog, too, with respect and gentleness. Even a dog that is exceptionally good-natured is no stuffed animal whose ears or tail you can pull to your heart's content. Dogs feel pain, and they know very well whether they are being treated lovingly. Any dog, but especially a puppy, must have periods of quiet, and dogs need plenty of sleep.
- Having a dog is not all pleasure and play. Dogs must be fed, looked after, and groomed. Children should help with these chores and occasionally take over some of them. When children are old enough, they can take the dog for a walk or stay home with it occasionally as "dog sitters." They can also assist in the daily grooming. This not only relieves the parents but is also an ideal means for deepening the friendship between dog and child. Preschool children should never be left alone with a dog, even if the dog is still a puppy.

Dogs and Babies

If there is a baby in the family, it should not be kept in complete isolation from the dog. Otherwise, the dog might get the mistaken idea that the carefully "hidden" little human is not part of the pack (the family). A grown dog might try to drive away the supposed "intruder" by nipping at it. Stories of such cases crop up periodically, but on closer examination, it usually turns out that the dog had been treated inappropriately. Avoid this mistake, and let baby and dog get acquainted with each other.

Talk in friendly tones as you lead the dog up to the baby. The dog will want to examine the little human in its own way, that is, by sniffing. Let it have its way, but do not allow it to lick the baby. Do not be overly worried about germs because the danger of transmitting a disease is practically nonexistent with a clean, dewormed, and properly vaccinated dog. Even if a member of the family is pregnant there is no need to move the dog out of the house, but do make sure to take it to the veterinarian to check for parasites, especially tapeworms, about six weeks before the baby is due.

If you give your dog a chance to get acquainted with the baby in its own way, it will accept the infant as belonging to the family and may even try to protect the baby as the weakest member of the pack. If you do not give any cause for jealousy by neglecting the dog in favor of the baby, everybody will coexist peacefully. Any child growing up with a dog will remember the experience fondly for the rest of his or her life.

How to Get Your Dog Used to Other Pets

If you already have a pet and are getting a dog, you should be aware of the following. In the case of a puppy, the two pets will adjust to each other relatively easily if you let them approach each other gradually but, at first, under supervision. If the new dog is already fully grown, you should be more cautious. Do not try to force things. If the antipathy between the two animals is so great that peaceful coexistence seems impossible despite your most patient efforts, you may have to give up. You may have to accept that the two will probably never get along, even after an extended period of living together under the same roof. That is why I would advise you to make this test before you actually buy a dog.

If you are dealing with a cat and a dog–two animals whose body languages are miles apart–the process of adjustment can be eventful to say the least, especially if both are fully grown. Cats and dogs that have lived in the same house for some time do take on a "house smell" that is imperceptible to our senses but is responsible for their accepting each other eventually. A puppy and a kitten will get along fine, learning enough of each other's "language" in play. Occasionally they may become so attached to each other that they choose to sleep together.

If you already have pets that belong to the natural prey of canines, such as hamsters, guinea pigs, or rabbits, extra caution is in order. These animals should be kept in secure cages and be let out only when the dog is not in the same room. The same is true if you have a parakeet that flies around the room from time to time. There is no guarantee that your dog will not go after it, even if it is normally trustworthy. Once its hunting instinct is awakened, there is no stopping it, and neither words nor punishment has any effect. See to it that no such situations arise. If you have children–who are sometimes forgetful and careless–you may be better off enjoying the pets you have without adding a dog to the household.

I say all this even though I have witnessed the most amazing friendships between different animals. I once knew a dachshund that fell in love with a dwarf rabbit, and I have seen a hunting dog protect a helpless chamois kid and even sleep with it. I could go on listing examples of this kind, but they are still exceptions to the rule.

A Second Dog

If you want to introduce a second dog into your household, you should be prepared for some difficulties at the beginning, especially if both dogs are already mature. They will have to test their strength until it is clear which is the top dog and which will have to assume the role of underdog. This competition for rank

Hunting and stock dogs.
Above left: Münsterländer; above right: pointer, pointing
Center left: Irish setter; center right: golden retriever.
Below left: Bernese mountain dog; below right: collie, tricolor.

will be resolved happily only if you always treat the dogs with patience and, above all, with absolute impartiality. The most important thing is to always feed both of them at the same time and to give each its own dish.

As long as the newcomer is still a puppy—up to four months old—its age acts as a natural barrier to conflict. Its position in the relationship is clearly defined, and life with an older dog is unproblematic.

The only time you are likely to encounter insurmountable difficulties is if you want an older female to accept another female. In such a situation you may run into an antagonism that will cause constant quarreling and fights. If you are absolutely determined to have two female dogs, you had best get female puppies from the same litter because littermates usually get along well together.

Before You Decide to Breed Your Dog

Anyone who wants to raise puppies should be aware that breeding purebred dogs is no simple matter and that it is unlikely to make anyone rich. Breeding dogs demands a sense of responsibility, a knowledge of genetics, lots of time and effort, and a good dose of luck. There are plenty of more or less successful breeders already. Superfluous and incompetent breeding should be discouraged in the interest of preserving the health and purity of our dog breeds. No one wants to see our essentially healthy purebred dogs degenerate into nervous and physically unfit creatures. Let me add another point: Every year all over the country innumerable dogs are abandoned. There is little you and I can do to prevent this kind of inhumane behavior, but we can do our part to see that dog breeding is pursued responsibly and on a limited scale.

Hunting dogs: wirehaired dachshund (left), and German wirehaired pointer (right).

When Your Bitch Comes in Heat

A female dog enters her first heat period (or estrus) between seven and ten months of age. Although the heat lasts from three to four weeks, the bitch is receptive to males only during a five-day period at the height of the estrus cycle. Chances for conception are greatest from the ninth to the thirteenth day after the onset of heat. A bitch should not be bred until her second or third heat period, nor should she have a first litter after the age of four years, because complications are more likely at a first birth in animals that are either too young or too old.

Male dogs reach sexual maturity when they are about one year old. They are then ready to mate at any time. Since the penis of a dog reduces to normal size only slowly after copulation, the mating pair stays locked together for about fifteen minutes after the act. Even if the mating was unplanned and undesired, it is pointless to try to force the dogs apart then because insemination will in all likelihood already have occurred. Also, such violent interference can cause serious injury to both dogs.

Heat can occur at any time of year, but it normally sets in about every six months. In the spring and fall there inevitably seem to be bitches around whose scent drives all the sexually mature male dogs in the area to distraction. This is also a trying time for dog owners.

Try to keep your animals under good control. Signs of sexual interest in male dogs are a sudden increase in appetite, extreme restlessness, whining, howling, and a constant eagerness to run off.

For owners of female dogs, there are three ways to prevent the birth of undesired puppies:

- *Spaying* or *sterilization* of the bitch, which means the removal of her ovaries and uterus, an operation that is utterly routine in this country.
- *Hormone treatments* (injections administered by the veterinarian), which, if continued over a long period of time, can cause health problems.
- *Isolation from all male dogs* for as long as the heat lasts. This no doubt involves some inconvenience, but it is, and always has been, the safest method of contraception.

If your bitch is not of a large and unwieldy breed, I would suggest that you carry her in and out of the house (about 30 yards) when you take her out for walks during the period when she is so irresistible to males. This may sound like too much of a chore, but your house is much less likely to be besieged and beleaguered by dogs if the bewitching scent line stops short rather than leading right to your front door. To aid you in your battle, there are also scent-inhibiting sprays and, better yet, chlorophyll tablets that you can buy at pet stores. To keep the ovulating bitch from spotting your home, you can put a pair of special panties on her during these critical days.

If you do decide to breed your dog, you should join a dog club of the appropriate breed (Addresses, page 132) early enough to get all the pertinent information in time. These clubs can also furnish you with any official papers you need, and they are ready to assist with advice, both practical and theoretical, when whelping time approaches.

Whelping

The average gestation period lasts sixty-three days. To figure the expected whelping date, you add two months and two days to the date of mating. It is not uncommon for puppies to appear a few days earlier than anticipated, and it is a good idea to watch your bitch carefully from the fifty-ninth day on. Restlessness and refusal to eat are the first sign that whelping time is near. Then the teats begin to swell and secrete a few drops of milk. When the body temperature drops from 102 to 99°F (39 to 37°C) and when the first contractions set in, it will not be long before the first puppy is born.

You should make advance preparations for the whelping well ahead. The whelping bed should be ready in a warm, quiet spot well protected from drafts. An infrared lamp mounted nearby will supply extra warmth should it be needed. Buy a whelping box

A dam nursing her puppies. By kneading rhythmically, the puppies stimulate the flow of the milk.

(available at pet stores; see drawing on page 24), or spread several layers of newspaper on the floor, put an old blanket on them for padding, and cover this with some clean, soft cloths that can be replaced if they get dirty.

About two weeks before the anticipated date of delivery, you should introduce the bitch to this new bed. You should also consult your veterinarian and have the telephone number handy. And, if you ask, the kennel where you bought your dog and your dog club will be willing to help in whatever way they can.

About one to three hours after the labor pains begin, the water breaks and the first puppy is born. The others usually follow at fifteen- to twenty-minute intervals. There may be six to eight, or even more.

After breaking the amniotic sac, the dam bites off the cord and then licks and massages the newborn pups to start them breathing. If the dam fails to perform these instinctive actions, the human attendant must step in and tie the cord, rub the puppy dry very gently, free the nostrils and throat of amniotic fluid, and, finally, get the puppy to nurse.

False Pregnancy

The theory that female dogs that have not had at least one litter of puppies are more likely to get sick is false, but it is true that these dogs suffer from false pregnancies more often than those that have been allowed to have puppies. The symptoms of false pregnancy are practically identical with the signs of real pregnancy. About eight weeks after the heat period, the teats swell up and secrete some milk. The bitch is restless and acts unpredictably. At this stage she can nurse and be a foster mother to orphaned puppies. If there are no puppies for her to take over, she will adopt substitute babies in the form of toys, bones, and so on, which she will gather and "mother." Unfortunately, there is no drug to alleviate this condition, but there are some things you can do to help her over this difficult time. Get her a number of toys, such as stuffed animals (page 25), to play with and lavish her affections on. Add plenty of vitamins to her food to help her body get over the physiologic manifestations of this critical period. During a false pregnancy, a dog also needs to be treated with special empathy. Her hunger for affection and her need to belong are greater than ever.

Taking Your Dog Along on Trips

Dogs, with very few exceptions, are social creatures. They have evolved in nature to live in packs, and their attachment to other members of the pack – in our day, to their human families – is as strong as it was among their forebears. A dog that has to live in separation from its companions can suffer such psychic pain that it will grow more apathetic by the day, refuse to eat, and eventually become sick.

Dog owners who would like to go away on vacation are faced with the problem of what to do with their pet while they are away. Not everyone has friends or neighbors who are willing to look after a pet. Boarding kennels are not always a good solution because some dogs that are used to being part of family life are simply miserable when cut off from life as they know it and locked up in an unfamiliar pen.

If you plan well ahead and are willing to make some concessions in choosing the destination of your trip, you can probably find a solution acceptable to everyone concerned. You can find hotels, motels, and guest houses almost everywhere that allow pets. Some travel agencies even offer "tours with your dog." If you decide in favor of a vacation that includes walks and hikes, the time spent away from home may well turn out to be happier and healthier for the entire family than if you had left your four-footed friend behind.

Temporary Adoptions

If you simply cannot take your dog along, ask the people at the kennel where you bought your dog whether they could help you out. Many breeders are willing to take in temporarily dogs that came from their kennels. In some cities, a less well-publicized alternative exists, namely, temporary adoptions. Shelters or clubs collect addresses of people who are willing to look after a pet for a while. If you obtain such a list of addresses, you can then get in touch with one of these people and discuss the details. Perhaps you can offer to reciprocate at some future date and thus establish a useful and friendly relationship.

Travel by Car

A dog's place in a car is in the back seat. Large dogs are best stowed away in the back of a van that is separated from the front by a net. Make sure the animal is not exposed to any drafts because this can cause conjunctivitis, tonsillitis, or ear infections, all of which are unpleasant and take time to heal. It goes without saying that you should make rest stops at least every two hours so that the dog can get some relief and exercise. Do not forget to take along a bottle with fresh water and a water dish because you might get stuck in a traffic jam, and on a hot summer day a car quickly turns too hot for a dog.

Before you leave home, you can give a tablet for motion sickness to a dog that is not yet used to traveling and tends to vomit (get a prescription from your veterinarian).

Travel by Train and by Air

Dogs may travel by train, but find out in advance; you may perhaps have to compromise with respect to choosing your vacation destination. Small dogs travel in a basket or carrier. Large dogs, however, are often allowed on trains only if they travel in a shipping crate in the baggage car. You must deliver them there and pick them up again when your reach your destination.

If you plan to travel by air, you should consult the airline in question about their regulations for pets. In some cases, a small dog is considered hand luggage and travels free of charge. Large dogs travel in shipping crates in pressurized cabins of the luggage compartment. Some airlines charge a certain percentage of the air fare per kilogram of weight. Dogs are usually not permitted on charter flights. You can see how important it is to ask well ahead for detailed information from airlines, travel agents, or tour organizers.

Necessary Items for a Trip

- An international certificate of vaccination and a current health report signed by your veterinarian. Vaccinations must predate the date of departure to a foreign country by at least three or four weeks but no more than one year. That means a visit to the veterinarian at least four weeks before a planned trip abroad.

- Food and water dishes. Do not forget a bottle of fresh water if you go on a trip by train or car.
- Sleeping basket and/or blanket. Collapsible travel beds are most practical.
- A leash and, in areas with rabies epidemics, a muzzle.
- A dog brush and comb and some disinfecting powder.
- A first-aid kit (your veterinarian will gladly help you decide what should be included).
- Canned and dry dog food if your dog's habitual fare is not likely to be available where you are going. If your dog is not accustomed to commercial dog food you should introduce it before you leave by gradually substituting increasing amounts for its normal, homemade fare.

You can obtain information on specific regulations governing the entry of animals into various countries by writing to automobile clubs and the consulates of the countries in question and by asking your veterinarian.

Training Your Dog

All our modern dogs, whether diminutive Pomeranians, poodles, or Great Danes, are descended from wolves and are still heir to "wolfish" instincts, even if some of these have been relegated to the realm of the subconscious. To survive, wolves must live according to strict laws. Each family of wolves forms a pack within which every member has its assigned place in the ranking system. The leader of the pack, the strongest and most intelligent animal of the group, is the accepted and absolute ruler. Its will is the law to which all the other wolves submit unconditionally.

As your dog's master and leader, you can train it to become an obedient companion and member of the household if you (like the lead animal of the pack) make use of your dog's innate mentality. A young dog will accept and subordinate itself only to a strong (that is, higher ranking) leader, in this case, you. This means that you must use consistent discipline to train your dog but never resort to harsh physical punishment. That would achieve just the opposite of what you want, for lead wolves never "beat" their followers. Patience, praise, persistence, and, if necessary, sternness – these are the qualities you need to display in your dealings with your dog, and they are the foundation of successful training. Only a well-trained dog is a source of unmixed pleasure, a dog whose good behavior you can count on all the time and wherever you are.

Housebreaking Your Puppy

Your first delight at having a puppy may soon be somewhat diminished by the sudden appearance of a puddle. Few puppies are housebroken by the age of eight to ten weeks. How could they be? Up to this point they have lived together with their littermates in a pen where they relieved themselves wherever and whenever they felt the urge. Why should your living-room carpet, which is softer and more absorbent that the old corner in the pen, be off limits?

A puppy, which is at the developmental stage of a baby, cannot possibly understand this. It is both pointless and unjust to punish it for not knowing what it has not yet been taught. It does not do any good to make a big deal of the incident and rub the offender's nose in the puddle, and it is too late to rush the puppy outside now that the accident has happened and the bladder is empty.

All you can do is keep a constant eye on your dog and take it outside, preferably to the same spot every time, whenever you notice the slightest sign that it might be about to empty its bladder or bowels. With a young dog, this means taking it out first thing in the morning, after naps, and after it has eaten or drunk anything. A typical sign that it is time is when it starts wandering around restlessly or turning in circles while sniffing and perhaps pawing the ground and whining.

If you keep a good watch from the very beginning and get the dog to the accustomed spot outdoors before the need strikes, as well as at regular intervals (every two or three hours), it will soon grasp what is expected of it. Once it starts heading outdoors on its own initiative and letting you know when it needs to go, it will not be long before it will be completely housebroken. Praising it each time it has done what was expected helps reach this goal more quickly. Of course, this takes a lot of time and patience, because puppies need to relieve themselves at least six or seven times a day. Once you have helped your young dog over this phase you will be rewarded by not worrying any longer about puddles, certainly not as long as your dog stays in good health.

While we are on this subject, there is one more thing all dog owners should bear in mind: taking your dog for a walk does not mean letting it relieve itself wherever it pleases. Though some of the fees you pay for keeping a dog may be used to clean up streets, you and your dog are in no way entitled to impinge on the rights of others. Only if you behave with consideration toward others can you expect them to put up with your dog. Everyone who keeps a dog shares in this collective responsibility of dog owners, and we should all remember that.

So, please curb your dog, and do not let it relieve itself in the middle of the sidewalk. If the road has no shoulder and there are no trees, you may have no choice but to let the dog use the curb. In parks, too, the paths must stay free of dog excrement. Well-trained dogs will almost always manage to find a place that gives offense to no one. If all dog owners were just a little more thoughtful, the relationship between our dogs and the rest of humanity would improve dramatically, and endless complaints about "dog messes" would cease.

Basic Dog Obedience

The purpose of dog obedience is not just to make life with a dog more pleasant; training is important primarily for the well-being and safety of the dog. Only if it is well-trained will it be safe from the dangers that surround it everywhere. How quickly a careless dog can get hit by a car or cause an accident by crossing a road heedlessly. In the countryside, too, a disobedient dog that leaves the vicinity of its master faces danger. Dogs found roaming or chasing game can legally be shot by the warden.

That is why you should start training your puppy as soon as it joins your household. At this early stage, you can utilize its juvenile pleasure in play. The more fun it has playing with you, the more eager it will be to learn. It should have mastered the following lessons by the time it is grown to full size.

- It must be completely housebroken and respond to its name.
- It must distinguish between the following commands and obey them: come, lie down, sit, stay, and no.
- It must be able to "heel" without pulling on the leash.
- It must behave properly indoors, not only at home but also in unfamiliar places (restaurants, for instance); that is, it should neither race around wildly nor yap constantly.
- It must behave properly both in your car and in buses, trains, and any other vehicle. It should not jump out of an open car door unless it is told to (always keep it on a leash).
- It may not beg and should not accept any food from strangers.

To achieve these goals, it is important always to use the same commands. It does not really matter which words you choose as commands, but it is crucial that you stick with the established command word. The first things your dog must learn, however, are to understand you, not to beg, and to walk properly on a leash.

"His Master's Voice"

Your dog loves to hear you talk, especially if you tell it nice things, and you should do this often. At first your words will have next to no specific meaning to it, but it will listen attentively to the tone of your voice and will instinctively interpret it correctly. Although our language is totally unlike its own, it will gradually associate certain events or experiences with specific sound patterns, and later even learn some words – if they are repeated often enough – and respond to them "intelligently." This is the way a dog learns to recognize its name, to tell the difference between praise and rebuke, and to obey the commands so cruçial to its education (page 48). It will soon recognize the word "walk" and will start a little dance of anticipation whenever you say it. This innate talent for comprehension is what facilitates the training of your dog. It will grasp the meaning of a sharp "no!" quickly and without previous practice if it is spoken immediately after it has done something wrong or, better yet, while it is doing it. With a dog that is normally spoken to in quiet and gentle tones, a stern word will usually have the desired effect.

Do Not Let Your Dog Beg

If you cannot sit down to a meal without being pestered by your dog's persistent begging, you have no one to blame but yourself. Feed your dog before sitting down to your own meal. Never give it any treats from your table, and insist that your children and guests also refrain from doing so. Only if you follow these rules can you expect to have a well-trained dog that will not be a nuisance even if you take it along to a meal out or let it be present at a celebration at home.

An animal that is used to being fed at specific times and eating only from its own dish is not likely to beg at the table. This is also the only way to ensure that it will not let itself be bribed or even poisoned by strangers.

Punishment – When and How

If an energetic "no!" goes unheeded, you will have to resort to a smack on the rump. Never use your hand or the leash for this. Your dog perceives your hand as something positive that feeds, pets, and grooms it. The best instrument is a rolled-up newspaper that makes a special impression with its loud noise. In a pinch you can use a soft broom or something of that sort. The effectiveness of the gesture depends less on its unpleasantness than on the element of surprise. The punishment should follow immediately on the heels of the misdeed; otherwise, the animal has no idea what it is being punished for. A dog that is frequently hit by its master's hand may develop such a phobia toward human hands that it will shy away from them and make further training and grooming or touching of any kind difficult if not altogether impossible.

Another trick for disciplining that works particularly well is one that wolf mothers use. Grab the puppy by the scruff of its neck, holding on to as much skin as you can, and shake it vigorously as though you were shaking the dust out of a mop, but without lifting it off the ground. If this is accompanied by a stern "no," it will make quite an impression, and the puppy will soon get the idea that it did something wrong.

Do not forget: Success in dog training is not achieved through punishment and physical abuse but instead through patience, repetition, practice, occasional rebuke, and, above all, through praise and rewards.

Walking on a Leash

A collar and a leash are crucial for the safety of a dog, particularly in the city, but the inexperienced puppy perceives these objects as shackles that can restrain its freedom of movement. In addition, the unfamiliar pressure on its neck frightens the puppy, and it reacts defensively by pulling on the leash.

To prevent this negative reaction to collar and leash, I suggest that you let your puppy get used to them by playing with them indoors. Put on the collar and walk the puppy around a little while, holding it loosely by the leash—but only after it has had a chance to sniff these objects at its leisure. If you do this in the spirit of play and repeat it periodically, the puppy will accept them fairly quickly and unproblematically. Once it has reached this stage, you can practice outdoors. One point is important: The dog should feel as little resistance as possible at the beginning. That is why a long leash with an automatic roll-up device (page 22) is good for these early practice sessions. Later, a leash of normal length (3 to 5 feet; 1 to 1½ meters) is adequate. The main thing is that your dog see the leash not as an instrument of torture but as a point of contact with you.

Once the dog accepts as a matter of fact that it will be put on a leash for walks, you can gradually get it used to busier streets where it can become familiar with car traffic and have a chance to meet other people and dogs. Before long, it will greet your reaching for the leash with excitement because it knows it is about to be taken for a walk. Dogs should not be kept on a leash all the time. Many of them have a great need for running and rapid movement. Give it a chance now and then to run off the leash, where this is possible (that is, where there is no traffic, no game, and no danger of rabies).

Taking Your Dog Along When Bicycling

Medium-sized and large dogs can be trained to run along next to bicycles either on the leash or off, but they must understand and obey the basic commands, particularly heeling. There is a slight complicating factor. Dogs taught to heel usually walk on the master's left, but when they accompany you on a bicycle ride it is safer for them to run along on your right. In the street, a dog running along on the left side of the bicycle would not only be in danger itself but also represent a hazard to other traffic. It is probably best not to practice this vigorous form of dog exercise on heavily traveled roads.

Take your dog along on a bicycle ride for the first time where there is no traffic. It will love this new "game" and may, in its enthusiasm, try to jump up on your while you are on the bike. Discourage this with an energetic "no." If this fails to have any effect, you may, for a short while, need the help of another person who will run a few steps ahead of the bicycle and to the right of it to attract the dog's attention. In this way, the dog will soon learn how to accompany you properly on bike rides.

Once you are both adjusted to traveling together at moderate speeds, you can try going a little faster to give your dog a good run on the loosely hanging leash. Do not overdo either your speed or the length of the excursion. The dog should never run so long that it is exhausted and dragged along behind. Depending on the size and breed, five or ten minutes of running and about thirty minutes to an hour of leisurely trotting are plenty. Unusually powerful dogs and whippets may have an even greater need for exercise. You should know your dog well enough to be able to tell when it begins to flag. If it is sick or not feeling up to par (animals, just like people, have their off-days), you should dispense with the excursion.

Dogs with advanced training or of unusually obedient disposition will behave properly when accompanying their masters on a bicycle or on horseback even without a leash. Within city limits, however, even when there is not much traffic, the dog must be kept on a leash.

Obeying Commands

"Come!"

After a dog has learned to walk properly on a leash (page 47), its next task is to practice obeying the command "Come!". After all, you will want to let your dog run loose once in a while (but only in appropriate places). You can risk this only after it has learned to return to you instantly when you call or whistle. This is not something that can be achieved overnight, and you should equip yourself with plenty of patience and some treats to be passed out as rewards. When your dog does what is expected the first time, you must lavish praise on it and reinforce its good behavior with a special bonus (but be careful not to exceed its daily calorie intake). It will remember these occasions and look forward to future practice. Once it has mastered the lessons, the concrete rewards can become smaller and gradually phased out. Eventually, a loving word of praise will satisfy it.

If your dog should decide to strike out on its own and later returns tired but happy, you should keep calm. If you scold or punish it physically at this point, the impenitent sinner will be completely bewildered. Its whole world will be upset, and it will reason something like the following: If I come home, they scold me and punish me, so it is better if I just stay away. It will be afraid, and that is just the opposite of what you want. Fear does not help anything. Dogs can understand being punished only if it happens while they are being bad or right after. Coming back is not being bad, after all, and the dog has long since forgotten that it went AWOL. So, you have no choice but to praise it for coming home. This is the only way you can be consistent, and that you must be. You will occasionally see a dog owner chasing after its dog while calling and whistling to it. This is a mistake, and you should never do it. Once the rascal sees and hears that you are taking its lead, it will feel all the more encouraged to keep running. If you stop, however, or start walking in the opposite direction, it will be startled, will stop, too, and will eventually come running straight back to you. If you praise or even reward it then, it will be less likely to play tag with you in the future.

I was able to teach this lesson easily to my cocker spaniel when it was still a puppy. I used to play hide-and-seek with it and stand behind a door or in a corner, where I would call "Come!". My playful little friend would come bounding up to me instantly and eagerly. It always waited for the word, even though it knew my hiding place perfectly well. It always got its well-earned "strokes," at first sometimes in the form of puppy biscuits, but most of all it enjoyed the praise I showered on it. I am sure it never felt that these sessions were mere "drudgery," and it never forgot what it learned.

"Sit!"

To teach the command "sit" you hold your dog on a short leash so that it must hold its head up. Then, when you say the word, you simultaneously press down on the rear end with your free hand so that it has no choice but to sit on its haunches.

A dog – in this picture a schnauzer – should respond instantly to the command "sit." This is something you should teach your dog while it is still a puppy.

"Lie Down!"

You proceed similarly when you teach the command "lie down." Push down on the dog's neck and rear end until it lies down. If you are dealing with a large dog, it may help if you pull the front legs forward while pressing down on the back. If it wants to get up right away, repeat firmly "lie down," and keep it from getting to its feet by pushing the back down with your hand.

Repeat this exercise two or three times a day, and once again, do not be stingy with praise and tangible rewards. Do not overdo the training, however, or your dog may lose its enthusiasm for learning.

Once the dog has learned the meaning of "lie down" and stays in place until you call "come," you should move away a little. You can then increase the distance a bit day by day. When it stays in its lying position even when you move out of sight, you both deserve to be congratulated on your achievements, you for your educational talents and the dog for its obedience. Never forget that each little step should be celebrated with a reward.

"Stay!"

When you need to put a leash on your dog because you want to cross the road or because there is some danger, the command "stay" is very useful. You begin teaching this comand by leading your dog on a normal leash. Be sure the animal is close at heel. Then you call "stay" in an emphatic voice, and pull back on the line so that your dog is forced to stop instantly. To keep it from sitting down (which it is supposed to do only when told to "sit"), you place your hand lightly against its belly (near the back legs). This way it will remain standing in the proper position. It will learn this lesson quickly, too, if you treat it with patience and reward it with praise and tangible tokens of appreciation.

"No!" and "Let Go!"

These are the commands to use whenever a dog is supposed to stop doing what it is doing or when you want it to relinquish something. A puppy should learn to accept early that at the command "let go" it should let you take away whatever it is playing with. At first it will growl and try to defend its "booty." This is just the way it behaved with its siblings, against which it had to assert itself to avoid being shoved into the background. In other words, it is a natural reaction, but you should not let it go unchecked. If you do, you will be sorry later, as when it picks up some splintery bone that you must get away from it so it will not be hurt. What could you possibly do if a grown dog simply refused to let go of its booty and defended it with strong teeth and perhaps a menacing growl? This example should make it clear how important it is that your dog learn this lesson early. You must convince it while it is still young that you are the stronger of the two and that it must give up without protest anything you ask for.

Practice this first with a toy your puppy is particularly fond of. Get your dog to play with the toy, and then take it away with a curt "let go!" when it loosens its hold on the toy. Praise its cooperation immediately, or reward it with a tidbit and return the toy. Practice with other objects, eventually even with its full dish of food.

Your dog will learn to accept this "game" or will at least not find it unusual to give up whatever it has between its teeth when told to do so. Never use force when practicing this exercise. To subordinate itself to a superior represents no sacrifice for a dog but is rather a natural reaction that it falls into because it accepts you as its "leader."

"Heel!"

All dogs should learn to heel when walking on a leash, and heeling without a leash is also important for large breeds and dogs used for work and for sport. Any dog must be kept on a leash on city streets and near game preserves. Even in less dangerous environments, where a dog could ordinarily run free, unexpected hazards may turn up. In such situations it is particularly important that your dog have learned to heel on command.

Practice by leading your dog on a short line. A little-used path along a wall or hedge is the best place. Here your student, held loosely at first and walking along on your left side, has no chance to veer away from you. Now you command "heel," and to signal to the dog what you want, you yank the line quickly and firmly every time you say the word, ideally when its head is right next to your left knee. At this point you should keep your dog from trying to bolt forward. A long, thin willow switch waved in front of its nose will discourage such attempts to break free. Remember, you only wave the switch; never use it to hit the dog. In the case of unusually large, strong, or difficult dogs, you may need a choke collar for this exercise. This can be made of leather or of rounded chain links that slide through the ring smoothly. What is important for the success of the exercise is that your dog feel the yank on the line clearly.

To try to keep the dog from pulling on the line in the future, it is good to practice at a slow pace at the beginning. If it does start pulling, use the command "sit," which it has already learned, and start the heeling exercise all over. This lesson must be drilled daily for some time, too. It is better to have several short practice sessions a day than one long one. Too long a session overtaxes the animal's patience and spoils its pleasure in the activity. Once your dog heels perfectly on a short line, you can continue the training on a longer one and eventually without any line at all.

Retrieving

Almost all dogs enjoy retrieving, that is, fetching an object on command. Of course there are hunting dogs with specialized skills in this area, but all dogs have a natural talent for retrieving.

Introduce the game like this. Roll or throw a solid rubber ball a few yards. If your dog has been watching, it will go after the ball instantly, leap on it as if it were prey, carry it around proudly for a while, and probably be most reluctant to give it up. If, in its excitement, the dog first turns a deaf ear to your "let go," wait a little while and then try again. This whole exercise should be more of a game than serious business because the dog must first get an idea of what it is all about. First, show it where the ball has bounced. When it has a firm hold of the ball with its teeth, walk away a few yards, and call to it several times, "Bring it here!" Then you squat down, pat the ground with your hand, and—before commanding "let go"—praise it lavishly. If it drops the ball or puts it down carefully, you praise it once again.

Some dogs grasp immediately what is expected of them, and others take some time to understand. Just about all of them think fetching is fun, except for a few lazybones, of which there are some even among canines.

Training in Special Skills

Once your dog has passed a course in basic obedience (that is, education for everyday life), it can go on to more advanced training. Many dog clubs, particularly those for working breeds, organize regular group practices and trials in which the participants are graded and their owners awarded certificates, ribbons, and cups.

This training beyond basic obedience is also advisable for many dogs that are not officially utility dogs, especially if you wish to have a reliable watchdog. The sport of the regular practice sessions not only helps release aggressive energy and sharpen the senses but also keeps animals physically fit.

Dogs belonging to officially recognized working breeds can be trained, depending on breed and regulations, to become guard dogs, hunting dogs with specialized skills, rescue dogs, dogs used by the police and the customs department, dogs for the blind, and so on.

The training of police dogs is usually organized into classes depending on the age of the animals (at least fourteen, sixteen, or eighteen

After a dog has gone through basic obedience training, it can go on to learn the skills of a utility dog. Even a stock dog, though born with the proper instincts, needs specialized training.

Greyhounds have a strong need for exercise. The greyhound is a stunningly elegant and fast racer, reaching speeds of over 30 miles per hour (50 kilometers per hour).

Training for a police dog includes jumping hurdles, tracking, and retrieving. Attacking is practiced, too, along with other exercises that test courage and obedience.

months), with a test for each class. The work is subdivided into the areas of tracking, discipline, and defense. In addition to "combat" training, during which a person wearing a protective sleeve plays the "aggressor," all the basic obedience exercises, as well as jumping hurdles, tracking, retrieving, dropping a prey, and many more skills, are practiced and tested by a trainer.

The necessary aggressiveness an attack or police dog must have presupposes responsible training that produces absolutely reliable obedience.

I would urge all dog owners, but especially those who want a dog who behaves properly in traffic or those interested in using the dog for sport, to join a dog club. Joining a club also opens up opportunities for friendly contact between members.

Dog Shows

Each year, dog shows of every description are organized throughout the United States, usually held indoors, especially during the winter. An extremely large and well-known show is the International Kennel Club Show held in Chicago. Forms of shows in the United States are as follows.

- The exhibiting of purebred dogs. There are hundreds of all-breed championship dog shows, as well as many separate specialty shows or championship events for single breeds.
- Often, specialty clubs work together for a combined show, such as an all-terrier show.
- All-breed shows often offer classes for obedience competition, the so-called licensed trials, at which obedience titles can be won.

Because there are many different dog shows, and great distances one must travel, it is customary to set up shows in circuits. This means that there are winter circuits lasting one or two weeks in (for instance) California and Florida and summer circuits in New York and

Illinois. It is even quite common that in different areas several shows are held simultaneously. There are also circuits that may have shows every other day, or shows on the weekends. So, if you are interested in dog shows, there are opportunities enough. The interest is still increasing, and even specialty shows where 200 and more German shepherds compete are not rare!

The dog shows usually commence judging at 9 a.m., and most shows are over by 7 p.m. To enter your dog in a show (time and place are always announced in club newsletters and specialized magazines), you must send in an application by the indicated date. The application should contain the name of the dog and the parents, the registry number and date of birth, and the addresses of the breeder and present owner. You must also indicate the class in which you wish to enter your dog, such as puppy, novice, open, utility, or competing champion. Copies of the pedigree, vaccination records, and health certificates (pages 16 and 58) are also required, as well as a nominal entry fee. Write for detailed information to the American Kennel Club or to the dog club representing your breed (Addresses, page 132).

Exhibitions in which purebred dogs are displayed in a ring for the judge to evaluate are of particular interest to breeders for their future work. Here the quality of their dogs is officially confirmed, and breeders can compare their dogs with other entrants.

The kind of exhibition and the rules applicable to a particular class govern how the judges rate the contestants. They go by the standards for each breed that define the ideal in terms of overall appearance, body structure, posture, and breed type.

If you are an ordinary dog owner without any ambition to breed dogs but still would like to have your dog assessed by an expert, you should enter your dog in a show when the opportunity presents itself. Do not go with great expectations, because the competition is stiff, the judges' standards high, and the number of winners obviously limited. In addition, such a venture subjects you and your dog to considerable wear and tear because of the travel involved and the hustle and bustle typical of shows.

You can also visit an exhibition without entering a dog. This gives you a good chance to become better acquainted with the different dog breeds, some of which you may never have heard of. The sponsoring organizations keep emphasizing that dog shows serve not only breeders' interests but should also promote general appreciation of dogs.

Surely you will not love your dog any less if it fails to win any prizes. It may not measure up in every respect to the standards of the breed, but remember that these standards are nothing more than human notions of perfection.

The Proper Diet

The Natural Diet of Dogs and What We Feed Them

Dogs are descended from predators (and carrion eaters) and live primarily on meat. However, their ancestors ate not only the muscle meat but also the partially digested food in the stomach and intestines of their herbivorous prey. In this way the canines received vitamins and minerals in sufficient quantities. These nutrients are just as important for our domestic dogs as they were for their wild ancestors. Dogs' lives have changed over the ages, and few dogs hunt for their food anymore, so we must see to it that they get adequate amounts of all the nutrients they need.

It is not a bad idea to buy food for one's dog at the butcher's but it is a mistake to buy only the very best cuts. An unvarying diet of heart, liver, and beef is too rich for a dog and supplies it with more energy than it can use. The result is that it gets fat and less physically fit, which will lead to problems of the heart and circulatory system and ultimately to a premature death. The fat content of food eaten by dogs should be no higher than 10 to 25 percent, depending on how active the animal is.

Fresh Meat – Raw or Cooked?

The food value of meat is the same whether you feed it to the dog raw or cooked. Meat always contains protein and fat. You should cook meat (especially pork)at least lightly, however. This is the advice of veterinarians, especially now that Aujeszky's disease (pseudorabies), a viral infection, has become more common. This disease represents no danger to humans; it affects primarily older pigs ready to go to market, and it is without symptoms so that it generally goes unrecognized. If meat from affected animals is fed raw, however, then the disease is passed on to the dog, which will die of it within one or two days because no effective treatment has yet been found.

Raw meat can also cause other sicknesses. *Salmonella,* a bacterial genus that causes intestinal disorders, thrives primarily in old meat, innards, and poultry. Salmonellosis can be fatal in young dogs up to six months old. Older dogs usually show no symptoms when they have this disease, but it can be communicated to humans. Raw meat is also a source of parasites. Bladder worms, or cysticerci – which are larvae of certain tapeworms and cause severe enteritis – are often present around the mouth of beef animals. Meat that has not been bled properly, such as heart, can cause diarrhea if it is fed raw. All these dangers can be avoided if you never give your dog raw meat.

Make sure your dog gets enough vitamins, minerals, and bulky foods by including cereal, rice, and vegetables in the diet.

Composing a daily menu that contains all the necessary nutrients in the right amounts requires a nutritional expertise that a new dog owner often does not have. It also takes more time and effort than simply opening a can of dog food. Another advantage of commercial dog food is that you do not have to worry about the diseases just mentioned.

Still, there are quite a few breeders who give their dogs nothing but fresh food because

A German shepherd has to be trained with utmost consistency. It needs lots of exercise and continued training.

they believe that only this kind of diet satisfies the natural nutritional needs of dogs properly. There are also dogs that do not take to commercial dog food readily. If puppies are introduced to it early enough, however, they will get used to it, and you save yourself the problems that can arise if the food your dog is accustomed to is not available on trips.

Commercial Dog Food

If you decide that buying, storing, composing, and preparing your dog's food is too complicated and time consuming, by all means use reputable commercial dog food. However, the Pet Food Institute is still trying to get permission from the Food and Drug Administration to use terms that are proper and understandable. Too many vague terms on the labels are still used to list the ingredients in a can or box ("meal," "by-products," or "digest of [meat] by-products"). So, use only reputable brands and remain wary of dog foods that list their ingredients improperly. You can use commercial food in combination with fresh vegetables and grains (see Additional Food, page 58). Dog food companies usually make four types of dog food.

- *Canned food* provides a nutritionally complete diet. It consists of a mixture of meats (muscle meat, tripe, heart, liver, and lung) and grains (rice, barley, oats, wheat, or corn) and contains all the important vitamins and minerals. Some canned dog foods have a higher carbohydrate content and others a higher percentage of meat and other sources of protein. (Read the label!) The latter type of food can be mixed with up to a third of whole-grain cereal, cooked rice, or cooked potatoes.
- *Semimoist food* is also nutritionally complete. Its moisture content of about 25 percent lies between that of canned and of dry food. Semimoist dog food is more concentrated than canned food. The need for liquid is covered partly by the moisture in the food and partly by drinking water. Since dry, semidry, and semimoist dog foods all contain less moisture than canned dog food, you must be especially conscientious about supplying your dog with fresh drinking water.
- The composition of *semidry* and *dry food* is basically the same as that of canned dog food. The main difference is that they contain less moisture. Some of these products contain as little as 20 or even 10 percent water, compared with the approximately 75 percent natural moisture of meat and plant matter retained in canned dog food. This makes dry and semidry foods considerably more concentrated and energy-rich.

By comparing the nutritional information given on the packages of various dog foods with the tables that follow (page 59), you can figure out how much food you should give your dog each day. On the average,
4 ounces (100 grams) of *canned food* contain about 380 kiljoules (=90 kilocalories)
4 ounces (100 grams) of *semimoist food,* about 1340 kilojoules (=320 kilocalories)
4 ounces (100 grams) of *semidry food,* about 1410 kilojoules (=335 kilocalories)
4 ounces (100 grams) of *dry food,* about 1550 kilojoules (=370 kilocalories)

Utility dogs.
Above left: wolfsspitz; above right: Siberian husky.
Center left: Doberman; center right: young giant schnauzer.
Below left: boxer; below right: Rottweiler.

There are also diet dog foods, but these can be obtained only from a veterinarian or a pet store.

Additional Foods

Whole-grain cereals, rice, fresh vegetables (except for cabbage and beans), fruit, and lightly cooked carrots are good additions to meat or canned dog food. You can also mix in an egg, some glucose, or some vitamins or calcium supplements as needed. By keeping the carbohydrates in the supplemental food low, you can help your dog lose weight if necessary.

Do not give your dog bones. Bones tend to pack the intestinal contents, which means that the dog becomes constipated. To keep their teeth and chewing muscles in shape, grown dogs (but not over five years old) can be given a hard veal bone now and then or a dog biscuit. Crusts of whole-wheat bread will also do. Best of all is a rawhide bone. Puppies love to chew, particularly when they are teething, and they can be given a little bit of dry food or a dog biscuit that is not too hard. These treats can also be used as rewards, which play such an important role in training. Do not forget to figure in these snacks in your calculation of the daily food amounts.

A healthy diet for adult dogs consists of about 50 percent protein, 40 percent carbohydrates, and 10 percent fat. Growing dogs should get between 60 and 70 percent protein, 25 to 30 percent carbohydrates, and 5 to 10 percent fats, plus vitamins and minerals.

With the help of the following tables, which are intended only as *guidelines,* you can determine how much food to give your dog daily.

Exact amounts are impossible to list because they depend not only on the age and weight of a dog but on whether its system uses the food efficiently and how much exercise it gets. The sex of the animal and the time of year also affect a dog's appetite. The tables indicate how much a physically normal male dog needs. Females, which are generally somewhat more delicate, eat less, but any dog that is very active will use up correspondingly more energy.

In the case of a young dog you should keep in mind the following. Puppies are growing animals going through the most important phases of their development. Their food and energy needs are, in terms of body weight, about twice as great as those of a mature dog. So, please follow the suggested amounts given in the feeding plan for puppies.

Feeding Plan for Puppies

The table shows the feeding plan for medium-sized breeds with an adult weight of about 28 to 33 pounds (13 to 15 kilograms), such as cocker spaniels, miniature poodles, and standard schnauzers.

For *small breeds,* such as dachshunds, pugs and toy poodles, the daily ration should be about half the kilojoule amount given in the table.

For *large breeds,* such as collies, Great Danes, and German shepherds, the amounts in the table should be doubled.

Another way to figure out the energy needs of your puppy is to weigh it and then multiply the number of kilograms (1 kilogram = 2.2 pounds) by the following values:
Up to 8 weeks, about 840 kilojoules or 200 calories

Feeding Plan for Puppies

Age of puppy	weight, pounds (kilograms)	Energy requirement per day (kilojoules)	Daily amount of food, including non-meat additions (see menu plans, page 60)
5–6 weeks	4.5–6.5 (2–3)	1930–2600	1 lb (440 g): A
7–8 weeks	6.5–9 (3–4)	2600–3260	22 oz (620 g): A/B
3 months	9–11 (4–5)	3260–4000	1 lb, 6 oz (700 g): A/B
4 months	15 (6.5)	4620	2 lb, 4 oz (1000 g): B
5 months	18 (8.5)	5670	2 lb, 10 oz (1200 g): B/C

Starting with the sixth month, the daily amount of food is gradually reduced to about 2 pounds (900 grams).
In the ninth month, you can start changing to an adult diet (see Feeding Plan for Grown Dogs).

Up to 4 months, about 590 kilojoules or 140 calories
Up to 6 months, about 550 kilojoules or 130 calories
Up to 9 months, about 420 kilojoules or 100 calories
After that you can start shifting to the adult diet.

Important: Do not forget to include the rewards for good behavior that take the form of food when you calculate the daily food ration.

Feeding Plan for Grown Dogs

You can find suggested menu compositions that add up to a healthy and balanced diet for dogs in the following table.

Feeding Plan for Grown Dogs
(4200 kilojoules = 1000 calories)

Dog's Weight, pounds (kilograms)	Energy requirement per day (kilojoules)	Daily amount of food: meat or canned dog food, including non-meat additions (Menu Plan D, page 61)
5.5 (2.5)	1,100	About 8 oz (200–250 g)
11 (5)	1,850	1 lb (440 g)
16 (7.5)	2,500	1 lb, 4 oz (570 g)
22 (10)	3,120	1 lb, 10 oz (740 g)
33 (15)	4,230	2 lb, 4 oz (1010 g)
44 (20)	5,250	2 lb, 12 oz (1250 g)
55 (25)	6,210	3 lb, 5 oz (1480 g)
66 (30)	7,110	3 lb, 12 oz (1690 g)
88 (40)	8,830	4 lb, 11 oz (2100 g)
110 (50)	10,440	5 lb, 8 oz (2480 g)
132 (60)	11,970	6 lb, 5 oz (2850 g)
154 (70)	13,430	7 lb, 2 oz (3200 g)
Up to 176 (80)	14,850	7 lb, 14 oz (3530 g)

Important: As in the case of puppies, you must figure in treats given between meals.

Feeding Times

When a dog is one year old, it no longer needs to be fed more than once a day. It should be given its meal around noon. If you continue feeding it twice a day, give it the first meal around noon and the second no later than 5 p.m. so that it will have plenty of time to digest and relieve itself before night.

A dog's food should be served at room temperature or lukewarm, never too hot or straight from the refrigerator. Always try to feed your dog at the same hour and in the same place. Whatever it not eaten within a quarter of an hour should be promptly removed to

Feeding Times

Age of puppy	Feedings per day	First meal	Last meal
2 months	2 for a nursing puppy	7 a.m.	7 p.m.
3 months	3–4	7 a.m.	7 p.m.
4 and 5 months	2–3	8 a.m.	6 p.m.
6 and 7 months	2	9 a.m.	5 p.m.
8–12 months	2	9 a.m.	3 p.m.

teach the dog that there is nothing to eat between meals and that begging is useless. If you let leftover food sit around too long, harmful enzyme activity and bacteria may develop.

The dog should always have available a dish of fresh (but not too cold) water. After eating, it needs to rest. If you want to take it for a walk, do so before the meal or wait for at least an hour afterward.

Diet of Commercial Dog Food and Nonmeat Additions

What follows are the suggested menu plans mentioned in the feeding tables (page 59).

Menu Plan A

A good two-thirds of the daily ration should be made of up canned dog food for puppies or of hamburger, chopped veal, or chicken giblets. The rest should be nonmeat foods (chosen to meet the energy needs of the animal), such as oatmeal with mashed hard-boiled egg or mashed banana, dry rolled oats mixed with some bouillon, or small amounts of dry milk or cottage cheese. Add briefly cooked carrots or spinach. Do not give more than one egg (lightly beaten or hard boiled) a week. If you feed your dog fresh meat, you should add calcium every day and 1 teaspoon of cod-liver oil or (preferably) vitamin supplements (Pervinal and Theralin, among others) twice a week. Consult your veterinarian if you are not sure what vitamins your dog needs. Special treats, which must be counted in the daily food ration, can consist of gristle, dry dog food, and puppy biscuits.

Menu Plan B

Two-thirds of the daily ration should be made up of canned dog food or of minced veal, lean beef, or heart (heart should be boiled briefly; the cooking liquid can be fed, too). One-third should consist of nonmeat foods, such as oat cereal mixed with water or cooked rice. Add to this some lightly cooked spinach, finely chopped raw lettuce, grated carrot, or half a grated apple. Once a week give 1 teaspoon of honey and one or two egg yolks. If you use fresh meat instead of canned dog food, add 1 teaspoon of cod-liver oil in the winter. If you give your dog no commercial food, start giving it a mineral supplement (many brands are available) at the age of ten weeks, and, at twelve weeks, also add a little glucose or honey. To keep the teeth strong and as a special treat (but without exceeding the daily food allowance), give dog biscuits, dry bread crusts, or cartilaginous bones.

Menu Plan C

About two-thirds of the ration should be made up of canned dog food or of beef, heart, gristly meat, or tripe. You can also use braised liver but not more than once a week. The last third is given in the form of nonmeat foods: cooked rice, uncooked wheat flakes, or thick rolled oats with lightly cooked vegetables (except members of the cabbage family, peas, and beans) and some parsley; also some grated raw carrot or apple. Add a pinch of salt. Or, instead of the vegetables, add some cottage cheese and mashed banana or grated apple to the wheat or oat flakes. Give one egg yolk per week. If you use fresh meat, add some honey or glucose every day, as well as a mineral supplement. Special treats (to be included in the calculation of daily food amounts): soft veal bones, some dry dog food, dry dark bread, or dog biscuits.

Menu Plan D

Find the appropriate amount of food for the weight of your dog in the Feeding Plan for Grown Dogs (page 59). Use either canned dog food or beef, heart, tripe, neck, or mutton. Do not feed liver more than once a week. Nonmeat additions (which have to be included in adding up the total amount listed in the table) are cooked rice, wheat flakes, or thick rolled oats (can be used uncooked as a thickener for juicy foods), combined with spinach, lettuce, grated raw carrots, or grated apple. Add a pinch of salt. Occasionally give some cottage cheese. Give no more than two to three eggs per week. For chewing, give rawhide bones and—if the dog will accept it—a whole carrot now and then. If you feed your dog only fresh meat and no commercial dog food, it will probably need calcium, phosphorus, and vitamin supplements. Ask your veterinarian. Special treats (to be included when you figure the daily allowance) are veal bones that are not too hard (not for dogs over five years old), some dry dog food, dry dark bread, and dog biscuits.

Feeding Puppies

Maybe the kennel owners where you bought your puppy have a special feeding plan they swear by and suggest you follow. If this plan is not based on commercial dog food for puppies, you can easily adapt the suggestions given in this book to their recommendations. Make sure you give your puppy something solid now and then to chew on and to keep the teeth clean. Old bread, a dog biscuit, some dry dog food, or some gristle is good for that. If the puppy is not fed any commercial foods, which contain all the necessary nutrients, it is important to supply the key vitamins and minerals in the form of supplements. Your veterinarian can advise you. As a general rule, all puppies that are weaned need calcium supplements until they are fully grown. This is important not only for the formation of bones and teeth but also for the proper functioning of the intestines.

The food dish should be heavy enough not to slide around on the floor and, for dogs with long, droopy ears, be narrower at the top than at the bottom. This keeps the ears from being dipped in the food every mealtime. A second dish with fresh water should always be available. It should be washed every day, and the water should be replaced frequently. Milk agrees with dogs only if it is diluted with an equal amount of water.

Feeding Grown Dogs

A dog is fully mature when its skeleton stops growing. On average, toy breeds reach adult size at twelve months and larger dogs at eighteen to twenty-four months. Often you can tell when a dog has reached maturity because its appetite suddenly diminishes. This changeover to a normal adult appetite reflects changes in the body as it ceases to grow. If the dog's lack of interest in food persists, and especially if it is accompanied by diarrhea, constipation, or vomiting, you should take the dog to the veterinarian.

A grown dog is fed only once, or at most twice, a day. The best feeding time is around noon. If you want to feed your dog in two installments, the second should be given no later than 5 p.m.

Amounts of Food for Old Dogs

When a dog gets old, it gradually eats less, but the food it gets should be especially nutritious at this stage because it now needs more protein and less fat and carbohydrate. You can figure on a reduction of needed calories of about 10 percent.

Fasting Days for Obese Dogs and Diets for Sick Dogs

A dog that is getting obese (weigh it more frequently, page 80) benefits from a day of fasting now and then. This helps clean out its system. Of course, you should be careful not to subject it to special exertions on this day. Make sure it has plenty of fresh water, because fasting should not mean going thirsty. The diet of overweight dogs should be lighter in fat and heavier in bulky foods (raw fiber) than that of dogs of normal weight. The other important factor is exercise. Take your dog for longer walks every day, and above all, follow the new regimen conscientiously and consistently! Fat dogs have a hard and usually brief life: Every move is an effort for them. The breathing, heart, and liver are affected, and eczema, diabetes, and other disorders often develop. Obese dogs lose their natural resistance, and if you do not do something about their condition in time, their life span is likely to be short.

There are canned dog foods for dogs with disorders of the heart, stomach, intestines, or kidneys. There are special diet foods for dogs with allergies and foods designed to improve an animal's general condition. All these special foods are available only from veterinarians and pet stores.

If Your Dog Gets Sick

Health problems in dogs can often be detected from external signs. To recognize and interpret these abnormal changes you should first familiarize yourself with a dog's physical structure and organs.

Short Lesson in Canine Anatomy

If you are just an ordinary dog owner without great ambitions to become an expert on canines, you do not need to know the name of every bone in your dog's body, but you should be familiar with a few of them, particularly those that keep turning up in the descriptions of individual breeds. Take the time to look at the drawings carefully.

The highest point of the upper back, which rises up between the shoulder blades, is called the withers. The distance from the ground (the dog should stand on a flat surface to be measured) to this point is the dog's size.

The upper posterior edge of the skull is called the occiput and is more or less pronounced in different breeds. The break in the line of the profile from forehead to nose is called the stop. The spinal column, which runs from the head to the tail, is made up of thirteen thoracic vertebrae, seven lumbar vertebrae, three sacral vertebrae, and twenty to twenty-three caudal vertebrae. Because of the spine's elasticity, dogs can move their hind legs far forward when running.

The hip joint, which is attached to the sacrum, connects the pelvis with the hind legs. If there is a constant strain on the pelvis, which is often the case with large and heavy dogs, this, combined with a wrong diet, can cause a joint disorder called *dysplasia of the hip.* This condition is found quite frequently in German shepherds, boxers, and terriers.

The hocks of the hind legs, which are made up of seven bones, are responsible for the

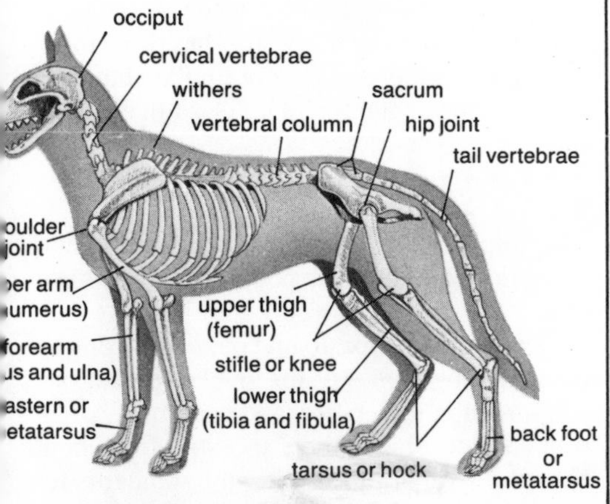

This drawing of a dog's skeleton shows the most important bones and joints that you should be familiar with.

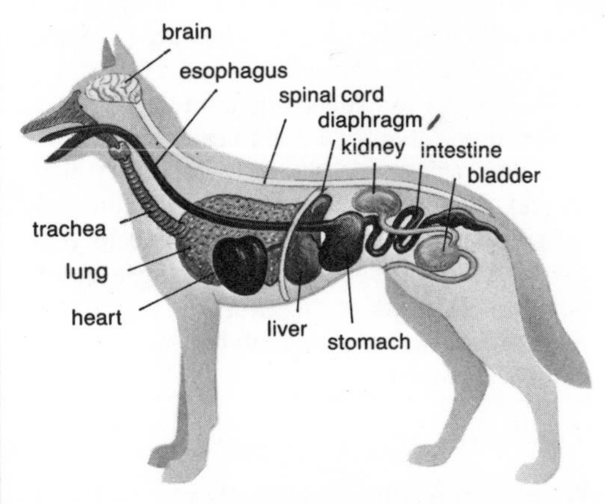

Internal organs of a dog. Heart and lungs are especially well developed and account for a dog's stamina and speed.

typical gait of dogs as well as for their jumping capacity. The feet are such that five pads and four nails touch the ground when the dog is walking. The fifth toe, which is sometimes present on the forelegs in vestigial form, has no practical function and is often, probably for esthetic reasons, removed right after birth. A few large breeds have this vestigial fifth toe on the back legs as well. It is called the dewclaw and is particularly undesirable in working dogs since it tends to get in the way and get caught and torn when the dog is running. For this reason, the fifth toe on the hind legs should be removed by the veterinarian in the first few days after birth. Larger, fully formed dewclaws can also be removed surgically later in the dog's life, but then anesthesia is necessary.

The energy needed for the functioning of the muscles, nerves, and circulatory system is provided by the basic components of the animal's food (carbohydrates, fats, and protein), most of which is converted into body heat. Of the internal organs, the heart and lungs are especially well-developed. They are responsible for a dog's speed and stamina. The stomach's capacity to expand and contract as needed makes it possible for a dog to eat a big meal only once a day. The bladder is also very elastic and allows for the accumulation of enough urine to satisfy a male dog's extensive need to mark territory (page 88). A dog's most important sensory organ is its extremely sensitive nose, which serves it as a kind of olfactory compass (page 91).

The Teeth

Whether miniature dachshund or Great Dane, all healthy adult dogs have forty-two teeth. Each half of the upper jaw has three incisors,

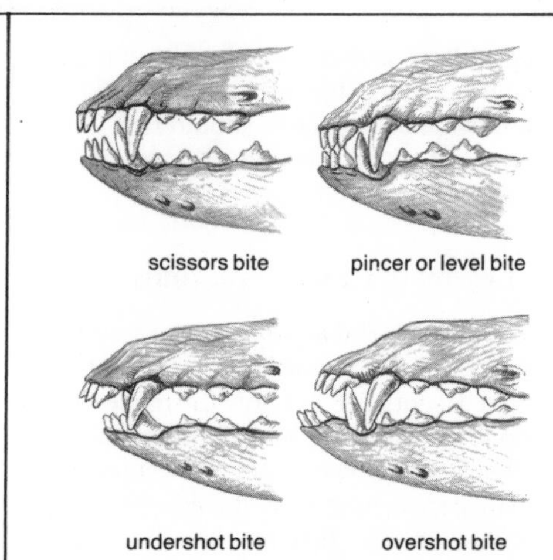

Different bites or dentations. In the scissors bite, the inner side of the incisors moves down over the outer side of the lower teeth. In the pincers or level bite, the edges of the upper and lower incisors meet exactly. In the undershot bite, the lower incisors protrude beyond the upper ones. In the overshot bite, the upper teeth protrude beyond the lower ones.

one canine, four premolars, and two molars; each half of the lower jaw also has three incisors, one canine, and four premolars but three molars. The dental formula for adult dogs, then, is

$$\frac{3 + 1 + 4 + 2}{3 + 1 + 4 + 3} \times 2 = 42 \text{ teeth}$$

The number of temporary or deciduous teeth is twenty-eight because puppies lack the molars.

There are four basic bite patterns in dogs (see drawing, above): the level or pincer bite, scissors bite, undershot, and overshot. Although according to their ancestry dogs should have the level or pincer bite, the standards for most breeds call for a *scissors bite,* and consequently many judges value it higher or "demand" it. In the scissors bite, which is found primarily in breeds with narrow skulls, the back edge of the upper incisors slides so closely against the front edge of the lower incisors that the teeth act like scissors when the jaws are shut. In aging dogs the teeth often shift from the scissors to a level bite.

In the *level bite,* which is characteristic of wild dogs, the sharp edges of the upper and lower incisors meet exactly when the jaws close.

An *undershot bite* is permitted as a characteristic of the breed in boxers, bulldogs, pugs, and Pekingese; in all other breeds it is considered a defect. In this type of dentition, caused by a shortened upper jaw, the lower teeth stick out beyond the upper teeth when the mouth is closed.

An *overshot bite,* in which the teeth of the upper jaw project beyond the teeth of the lower jaw, is a defect, as are irregularities in the placement of individual teeth. Particularly in utility breeds, the hereditary lack of premolars is common. X-rays taken at three months of age already reveal whether the beginnings of the normal number of teeth are present.

The Tongue

A dog's tongue has many functions. Not only is it used for lapping up water and food, cleaning the body, licking wounds, feeling objects, and expressing affection, but it also plays an important role in maintaining body temperature. Dogs, like humans, have sweat glands all over their bodies, but the body can be cooled sufficiently only if the airstream caused by panting moves over the wet tongue. To make full use of this cooling surface, dogs hang their tongues as far out as possible when it is hot or after vigorous exercise.

The Ears and Their Typical Shapes

The facial expression of all dogs is largely determined by the ears (page 66). Dog's ears come in many shapes, some of them manipulated (cropped) by humans. Starting with the pointed ears of the dog's ancestor, the wolf, we now distinguish among the following types of ears.

- *Pointed or prick ears:* the German shepherd
- *Cropped pointed ears:* Great Danes and Dobermans
- *Bat ears:* the French bulldog
- *Butterfly ears:* the papillon
- *Semi-prick ears:* the collie
- *Folded ears:* the fox terrier
- *Button ears:* the pug
- *Rose ears:* the English bulldog
- *Hanging or lop ears:* dachshunds and pointers

Should Ears Be Cropped and Tails Docked?

It is debatable whether it still makes sense today to crop dogs' ears (and in many breeds to dock the tails). In earlier times the ears of hunting dogs were cropped so that bears and wolves as well as smaller wild animals and rats could not sink their teeth into them as easily. The docking of the tails also was done as a safety measure against injuries sustained in tracking game through thick underbrush. Since most of our dogs are now kept as pets and neither fight with wild animals nor get much chance to get their tails entangled in

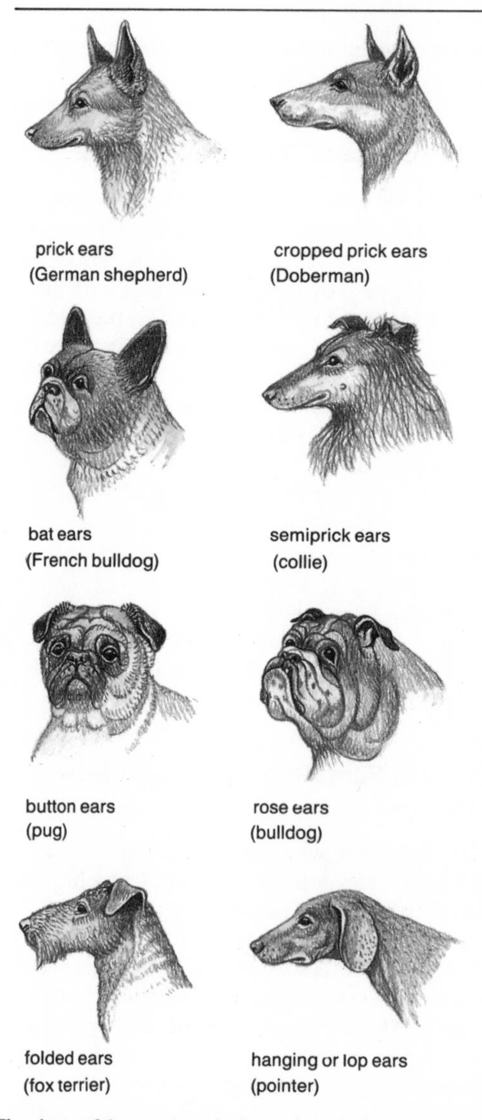

The shape of the ears largely determines the expression of a dog's face. In some breeds it is still customary to crop the ears.

thickets, these operations are justified only in dogs actually used for work or hunting. Nevertheless, ears are cropped and tails docked routinely even in breeds that have long since ceased to be used, or are used only very rarely, for hunting or for work that involves a risk of injury. Besides, the luxuriant coats that have been deliberately developed in many breeds would be much more of a hindrance for such work than a bushy tail. It is my opinion that the various breeds of dogs in their natural state, without alterations of ears and tails, offer enough variety to choose from and that we should refrain from interfering with Nature's work unless we have a good reason for it. Instead of amputating puppies' tails, breeders should concentrate on maintaining and improving the natural good qualities of their dogs.

Surgical corrections done for the sake of questionable ideals of beauty – I find contrary arguments unconvincing – are unnecessary and should be prohibited by law (except for a few truly justified exceptions).

I realize that by expressing these opinions I make myself persona non grata with a number of breeders and their associations, but I am not alone in taking this position. More and more people object to cropping the ears and docking the tails of dogs. In England, the paradise of dogs, as well as in the United States and Switzerland, these operations are performed now with far less frequency than they were even a few years ago. In these countries it has apparently been recognized that medical reasons for these procedures exist only in some individual cases. Cropping and docking done to conform to breed standards – to be performed under full anesthesia often in conformance with

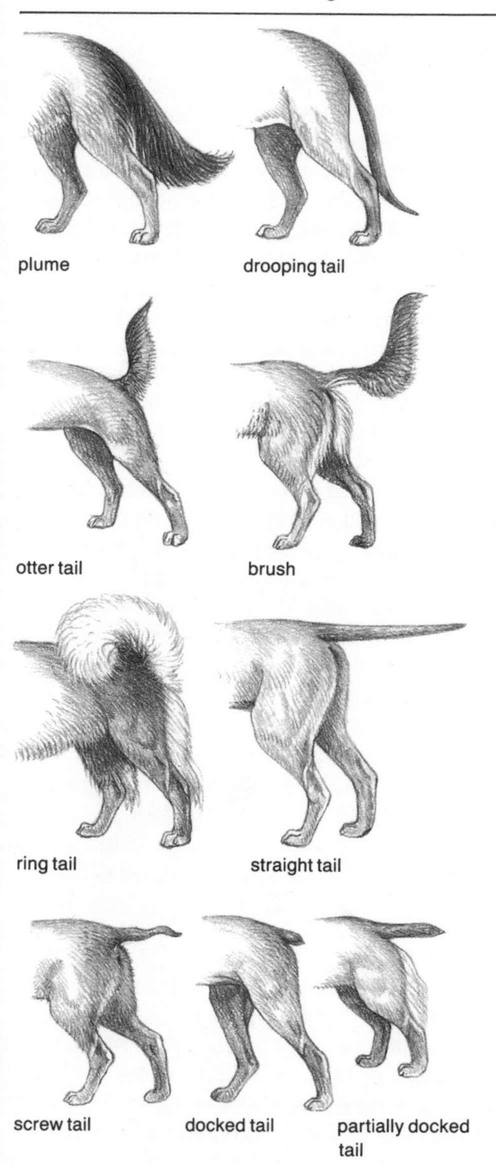

animal protective legislation – are still customary in the following breeds:
Cropping the ears in French mastiffs, bullterriers, and Great Danes.
Cropping the ears and docking the tail in boxers, Dobermans, schnauzers, Brussels Griffons, and miniature pinschers.
Docking the tail in Airedale terriers, Old English sheepdogs, cocker spaniels and some other spaniels, griffons, grosser Münsterländers, Kerry blue terriers, Irish terriers, poodles, Sealyham and Welsh terriers, German spaniels, Weimaraners, Yorkshire terriers, Stichelhaars, and – if the natural tail is overly long – short-haired, wire-haired, and long-haired German pointers.

Life Expectancy of Dogs Compared with That of Humans

The average life span of a dog is twelve to fifteen years. As you will see in the descriptions of individual breeds, however, some breeds hardly ever live beyond 10 years but others live up to 20 years. The simple formula for converting the age of dogs into human terms by multiplying the number of years by 7 is widespread but not quite accurate. Scientists

The tail, an important indicator of moods, is docked in some breeds (such as the boxer, doberman, and schnauzer) or shortened (such as the Old English sheepdog and spaniels).

have come up with the following table that reflects the facts more closely:

Age of dog	=	equivalent age of humans
2 months	=	14 months
3 months	=	3 years
6 months	=	5 years
8 months	=	9 years
12 months	=	14 years
18 months	=	20 years
2 years	=	24 years
3 years	=	30 years
4 years	=	36 years
5 years	=	40 years
6 years	=	42 years
7 years	=	49 years
8 years	=	56 years
9 years	=	63 years
10 years	=	65 years
11 years	=	71 years
12 years	=	75 years
13 years	=	80 years
14 years	=	84 years
15 years	=	87 years
16 years	=	89 years
20 years	=	95 years

Preventive Health Measures

If your dog gets sick, it should be treated by an experienced veterinarian because only an expert is able to diagnose a condition accurately and to prescribe the proper treatment. Do not rely on cures other well-meaning people suggest and do not try home remedies of your own because such delaying tactics might have disastrous consequences for your dog: Better to have made a trip to the veterinarian that turns out to have been unnecessary!

For the times when no veterinarian can be reached, on a weekend, for instance, you need some idea of what to do in case illness strikes. Also, there are some minor disorders that you can easily learn to deal with yourself. In any case, every dog owner should know something about the common dog diseases, how to recognize them, and what to do in an emergency. Let us first turn to preventive health measures.

Deworming

There is hardly a puppy born that is not already infected with roundworms. Conscientious breeders therefore deworm puppies (along with their mother) three times at ten-day intervals between the ages of two and six weeks. This procedure should be repeated in the puppy's fourth month and, to be on the safe side, when the puppy is eight months old.

When you take your new puppy to be vaccinated (below), you should have its stool analyzed to make sure no other endoparasites are present. Tapeworms are not as common in dogs as roundworms, but they do occur and must be combated promptly. Use only medications prescribed by your veterinarian, and make sure you give them in the proper dosage.

Since tapeworms use other parasites as intermediate hosts, laying the eggs in dog fleas, for instance, these parasites must be destroyed at the same time. Tapeworms also attack pigs and sheep, which is why the meat of these animals (and all other meat) should always be cooked before it is fed to dogs.

Hookworms and whipworms are also found in dogs, but they are less common in animals that are well cared-for than in poorly kept or neglected animals. Turn to page 33 in General Grooming to find out how to get rid of these pests.

Vaccinations

The first immunization, which should be administered when the puppy is seven to nine weeks old, is usually taken care of by the breeder. The next vaccination is due between the twelfth and fourteenth week and is usually the responsibility of the buyer. After that, yearly booster shots are necessary.

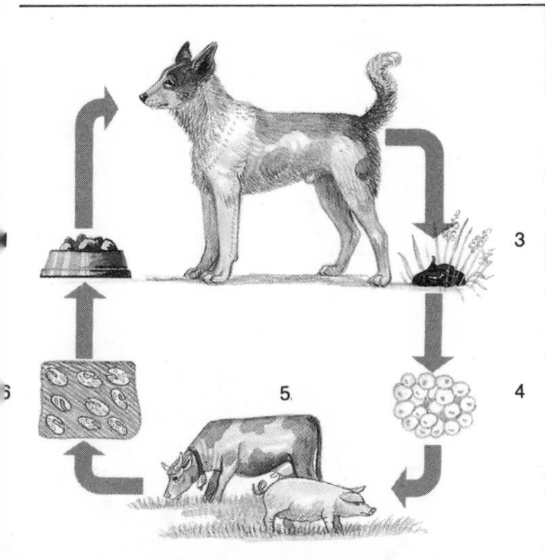

ife cycle of the dog tapeworm: Bladder worms, or ysticerci, absorbed in raw food (1) develop into tape- vorms in the stomach and intestines (2), where they lay ggs that are passed in the stool (3 and 4). In the intermedi- te hosts – cattle, pigs, and horses – which pick up tape- vorm eggs in their food (5), the eggs develop into bladder vorms that settle in the animals' livers, hearts, and lungs.

Ask your veterinarian for advice in good time. The veterinarian will explain to you what needs to be done and will enter all vaccinations in the international vaccination card you will have received from the person who sold you your puppy. This document, which conforms to the prescriptions of international dog associations, contains the record of rabies immunizations as well as official certificates of health and identity. These papers are necessary primarily for travel abroad but they are also required by some boarding kennels and for exhibitions. If there is any suspicion of rabies – which exists at the mere possibility of contact with an affected animal – authorities may ask for proof of vaccination.

To simplify the procedure of administering all the necessary immunizations, *combination vaccines* effective against distemper, hepatitis, leptospirosis, and rabies (page 72) have been developed. The vaccinations are harmless for both dog and owner since the vaccinated animal neither eliminates pathogens nor is a carrier of the disease, nor do the vaccinations cause symptoms of the disease.

How to Recognize a Disease

If your dog stops eating or drinks a lot more than usual, if it is lethargic and apathetic, does not like to be touched, has cloudy eyes, or if the consistency of the coat changes markedly, something is wrong with its general state of health.

Dull fur can be the consequence of a wrong diet. Perhaps it is not getting enough vitamins or trace elements or not enough hormones are stimulated. Worm infestations, liver and kidney diseases, and infections are also possible causes.

Loss of hair (when the dog is not shedding) and *breaking of hair* are either the result of old age or signs of fungus or parasite infestation.

Raising of the hair is not always just a sign of agitation. It can also be a sign of sores, pimples, or allergies.

A *dry, warm nose* is not necessarily indicative of illness, although the nose leather of a healthy dog is generally wet and cold. In case of doubt, take the dog's temperature (page 80).

Constant licking of the nose can be caused by a cut or other injury, a foreign object on the tongue, or by a cold.

Frequent swallowing and retching indicate a sore throat.

Sneezing and coughing can be caused by a foreign object in the mouth, nose, or throat, but they can also be early signs of a cold or of tonsillitis. If these symptoms are accompanied by a raised temperature, they should be considered possible signs of distemper (page 72).

Chronic coughing is a sign of a weak heart in old dogs. Consult the veterinarian.

Pale mucous membranes, visible in the lips and the inside of the eyelids, are a symptom to be taken seriously. They may indicate severe loss of blood or poisoning.

Teary eyes indicate conjunctivitis. Your dog either was exposed to drafts or has something in its eye. Rinsing with boric acid does no good. It is better to remove the discharge carefully with a clean, soft cloth or tissue, thus relieving the itching temporarily. If there is a discharge of pus from the eyes together with a fever, this may indicate distemper (page 72). Consulting a veterinarian is necessary in any case.

Constant tilting of the head suggests an inflammation in the ear canal or some disturbance in the brain. Unusual sounds and sound frequencies that are not audible to the human ear (some of them caused by television sets) can also cause a dog to tilt its head, which is of course harmless.

Shaking of the head suggests that there may be a foreign object on or in the ear. It may also indicate an ear infection requiring veterinary treatment.

If your dog is *dragging the rear along the ground,* it has an itchy anus that may be caused by a plugging of inflamed anal glands. Take the animal to the veterinarian.

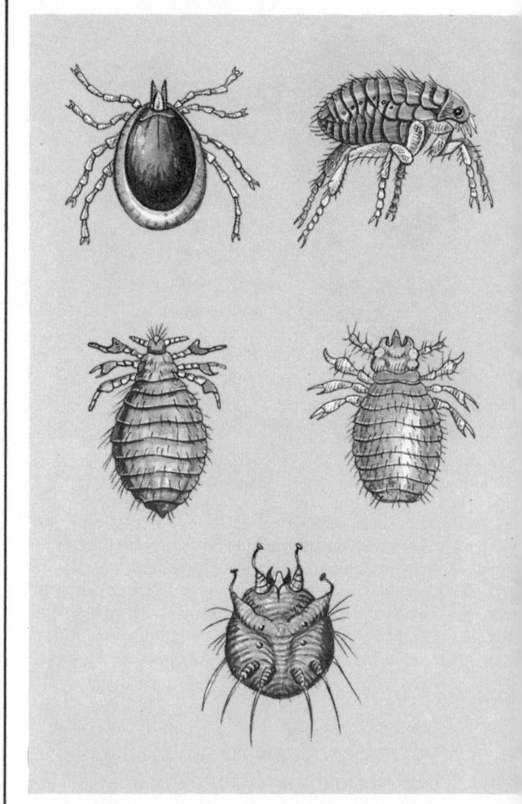

Ectoparasites of dogs.
Above left: tick; above right: dog flea; center left: biting dog flea; center right: sucking dog flea; below: mite, seen from below.

Frequent scratching may be caused by parasites in the fur—fleas, lice, or ticks. There are powders, sprays, and soaps available at pet supply stores to deal with this situation. If your dog keeps scratching one particular spot it may be because that place hurts. Take your dog to the veterinarian before the spot is scratched open and eczema has a chance to form.

Swellings in the mouth are usually the result of insect bites (bees or wasps). If the swelling does not go down soon by itself, the dog should be taken to the veterinarian.

A *fever* always signals an inflammation or an infectious disease. Call the veterinarian. Signs of fever are dull fur and eyes, apathy, and noticeably higher-than-usual body warmth (see how to take the temperature on page 80). Since fever is the body's natural defense reaction, it should not be suppressed right away, but if a fever lasts over a long period of time or the body temperature rises above 103°F (39.5°C), it is dangerous.

Vomiting is not necessarily a sign of sickness. If a dog has eaten too much or too quickly or has consumed food that is hard to digest, it will sometimes eat grass as a regurgitant in case of indigestion. Some dogs throw up when they travel by car or train. In these cases, a motion sickness pill given in good time before the departure has a calming effect.

Frequent vomiting, especially if accompanied by fever, indicates sickness. Only a veterinarian will be able to diagnose the cause accurately.

Diarrhea without fever can often be alleviated by feeding the dog thin black tea with a pinch of salt. Drinking is crucial because the loss of fluid caused by diarrhea must be made up for. A day of fasting usually brings relief. Follow this with a diet made up of some rice, cooked in salt water, mixed with some low-fat cottage cheese and pureed carrot to which you add two to three crushed charcoal tablets. If your dog refuses to eat this food, make it more appealing by mixing in a little braised hamburger. Diarrhea that does not clear up within 3 days and diarrhea that is *accompanied by fever* must be treated by the veterinarian.

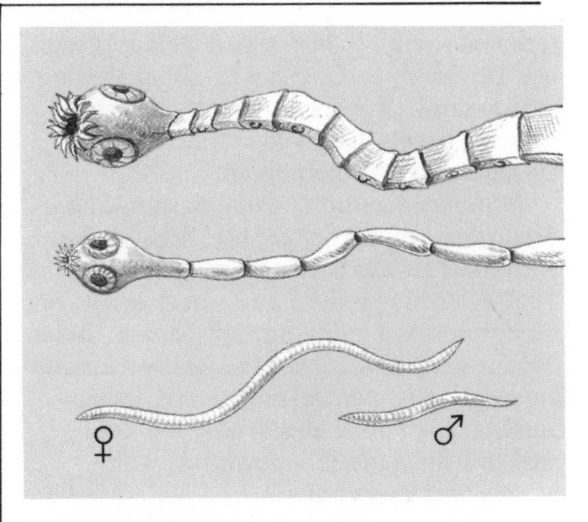

Endoparasites of dogs.
Above: tapeworm, communicable to humans; center: tapeworm, transmitted to dogs by fleas; below: roundworms.

Nervous stomach and *gastritis* are fairly common in high-strung dogs. Veterinarians have medications for relaxing nervous stomachs.

Excessive drinking may be caused by a diet that is too salty, or it may occur after vomiting or diarrhea. It can also be a sign of diabetes, nephritis, or—in females—of uterine inflammation.

Dark urine may be caused by certain foods or it may be a symptom of illness.

Blood in the urine is a real danger signal indicating a disorder of the urinary system and requires immediate attention from a veterinarian.

Blood in the stool, when accompanied by

repeated vomiting, may signal serious poisoning. Do not try to combat it by giving the dog milk to drink. It is better to force-feed some charcoal tablets dissolved in water and rush the animal to the veterinarian.

Intestinal parasites: Puppies should be dewormed before they are sold because they are almost always born with roundworms. The deworming is done by a veterinarian, who may prescribe a follow-up deworming. Older dogs develop a resistance to roundworms and are plagued by them less often. If diarrhea persists, it is a good idea to have the stool analyzed for signs of hookworms, whipworms, and tapeworms.

Cramps can indicate infections and acute metabolic disturbances as well as poisoning (poison bait for rodents and snails). *Muscle cramps* are often a hysterial reaction after excessive excitement.

Dislocation of the kneecap affects poodles primarily and is described in the section on disorders typical of certain breeds (page 79).

Lameness occurs mostly in older dogs,in which it is caused by chronic changes in the joints. Bruises and sprains are also possible causes, as are metabolic disorders and old age.

Eczema, which is a skin condition accompanied by itching, can occur on almost all parts of the body. Medication for it should be prescribed by a veterinarian.

A *growth* or *tumor* can be harmless or malignant, but since it may increase quickly in size and become more dangerous, you should have it examined by a veterinarian promptly. For more details, see the section on disorders typical of certain breeds (page 79).

False pregnancy and how to treat it are discussed on page 41 in Basic Rules for Keeping and Caring for Dogs.

Common Dangerous Infectious Diseases

Canine Distemper

Symptoms: Fever, diarrhea, coughing, and teary discharge from the eyes are the usual symptoms and, at a more advanced stage, cramps and abnormal movements.

If young dogs are affected by this viral disease, the case is practically hopeless. Even in older dogs, distemper usually causes incurable disorders of the nervous system.

There is now a new temporary vaccine against distemper with which puppies two weeks old can be inoculated; a repeat vaccination two weeks later is absolutely essential. After the twelfth week, permanent vaccines can be used.

Infectious Canine Hepatitis

Symptoms: These are fever, inflammation of the nasal and throat cavities, diarrhea, and a noticeable tenderness of the abdomen.

This viral disease, too, attacks dogs of any age, but puppies are most susceptible. As a consequence of hepatitis, dogs may develop clouding of the cornea, which quite often leads to blindness. If treated in time by a veterinarian with serum, antibiotics, and intravenous feeding, hepatitis can often be successfully combated, but the only sure protection is provided by a first immunization of puppies in their seventh to ninth weeks and again from twelve to four-

Medium-sized dogs.
Above left: standard poodle with a classic clip; above right: poodle, apricot colored.
Center left: dalmatian; center right: Kromfohrländer.
Below left: American cocker spaniel; below right: chow chow.

teen weeks, with booster shots every one or two years thereafter.

Leptospirosis

Symptoms: These are fever, listlessness, lack of appetite, and vomiting. Other frequent symptoms are weakness of the hind legs, tonsillitis, and disorders of the stomach, intestines, and kidneys. In serious cases, there may be jaundice, abnormal movements, and a foul odor from the mouth.

This bacterial infection is caused by various species of *Leptospira* and can be accurately diagnosed only by repeated blood tests. Yearly vaccinations offer the best protection.

Rabies

Symptoms: These are abnormal behavior, biting without provocation, paralysis, cramps, and difficulties in swallowing.

There is as yet no effective cure for this deadly disease, and any case of its occurrence must be reported to the health authorities. Rabies is caused by a virus that is transmitted in the saliva of infected animals, primarily by bites. Humans, too, are susceptible to the disease. Animals suspected of having rabies must be quarantined for observation by a veterinarian. Anyone who has had contact with an animal that might have rabies must receive shots immediately.

Puppies can be vaccinated against rabies at twelve to sixteen weeks, and booster shots should be given thereafter every year.

The cocker spaniel, which was used in the past for trailing and retrieving, still has a passion for hunting and likes to swim.

"Feline Distemper"

In the last few years a contagious disease caused by a virus related to that giving rise to feline distemper in cats has been observed. *Symptoms:* The first alarming sign of this disease is a bloody diarrhea that comes on abruptly. This is soon followed by vomiting, which can be bloody, too, as it gets worse. Then the dog becomes apathetic, refuses food, and suffers from serious dehydration. The temperature is usually only slightly higher than normal.

Because the disease takes such a rapid course, it is important to see the veterinarian as soon as possible, that is, as soon as the first symptoms are noticed. The more the dog's organism is weakened, the less likely is recovery. This sickness often ends in death, but if treatment is initiated early, especially with infusions and antibiotics, there is a good chance of recovery.

There is a vaccine to prevent feline distemper in dogs. The dog should be vaccinated twice, at a two-week interval. This vaccination is just as safe as the previously mentioned vaccinations, and it might save your dog's life.

Any dog owner, and especially anyone with a puppy, should be aware of these infectious diseases. There is no reason to worry about them if you make sure your puppy has had all the necessary basic vaccinations and if you are conscientious about taking your dog to the veterinarian for follow-up shots.

Are There Diseases Typical of Certain Breeds?

Veterinarians, geneticists, and other experts on dogs all agree that certain breeds of dogs are susceptible to certain diseases. This does not mean, however, that all dogs of a given breed are "fated" to get this disease. Still, it is a good idea for you to be aware of common difficulties so that you can be on the lookout for possible trouble spots in your dog.

The following table shows the illnesses or disorders for which different breeds have a propensity.

Disorders Typical of Certain Breeds

This enumeration of ailments – based on observation of dogs over a long period of time – is not meant to frighten you, as I have already said. It reflects statistical probabilities of what problems you might have to expect, and I have made this list so that you will know what to look out for in your dog.

Entropion
In this condition, which is found primarily in rough-haired breeds, one or both eyelids are inverted, creating itching and compulsive blinking. Later the irritation causes the cornea to become inflamed, and there is a slimy and pussy discharge from the eye. The condition may be congenital. Examine the eyes of a puppy carefully before you buy it. Palliative treatment sometimes works, but usually surgery is necessary.

Ectropion
Here an eyelid, usually the lower one, is everted or turned out. Again, the constant irritation leads to reddening and inflammation of the the eye and to tearing. The condition is sometimes congenital, but it can also be the result of paralyzed nerves or, in older dogs, of weakness of the lid muscles. In most cases surgical correction is necessary.

Glaucoma
Here the fluid cannot properly drain. This causes pressure on the eye, tearing, sensitivity to light, dilated pupils, reddened conjunctiva, sensitivity to touch, and disturbances in general behavior. If the condition is not recognized and treated in good time, permanent damage is done to the eye. It is therefore crucial that you consult your veterinarian promptly.

Keratitis
In this ailment, which can have a number of causes, the cornea turns bluish white. Sometimes a foreign body in the eye results in keratitis. Mild, antibiotic eye drops may help, but if there are major injuries (ulcers) or if the keratitis persists, consulting the veterinarian is mandatory.
Signs: These are sensitivity to light, blinking, tearing, opaqueness of the cornea, obvious pain of the eye.

Conjunctivitis
Particularly frequent in breeds with drooping lower eyelids. Often the so-called third eyelid becomes inflamed and swollen so that it protrudes from the inside corner of the eye, causing the hairs below to be caked with discharge.
Signs: These are reddening of the eye, teariness, pussy secretion, and sensitivity to light.
Treatment: Remove the discharge gently with a soft cloth or tissue. Consult the veterinarian.

Type of dog	Entropion, page 76	Ectropion, page 76	Glaucoma, page 76	Keratitis, page 76	Conjunctivitis, page 76	Disorders of sight and hearing, page 78	Impaired hearing, page 78	Inflammation of the ear, page 78	Allergies and eczema, page 78	Boils, page 78	Lumps and tumors, benign and malignant, page 79	Paralysis, page 79	Hip dysplasia, page 79	Dislocation of the kneecap, page 79	Unprovoked biting, page 79	Epileptic attacks, page 79	Eclampsia, page 79	Twisted stomach, page 80	Kidney stones, page 80
Old dogs		×					×				×	×							
– Short-haired										×									
Dogs with deep folds in skin										×									
Large, heavy breeds													×					×	
Rough-haired breeds	×																		
Water-loving breeds								×											
Toy breeds					×												×		
Basset hound																		×	
Beagle															×				
Bloodhound		×								×							×		
Boxer		×									×	×	×			×			
Chow chow	×																		
Collie; color, blue merle						×													
Dachshund										×	×	×					×		
– Color, harlequin						×													
Dalmatian							×												×
– blue-eyed puppies						×	×												
German shepherd									×				×					×	
Great Dane					×		×											×	
– Color, harlequin						×													
Newfoundland		×			×														
Pekingese				×	×							×							
Poodle			×					×						×		×			
Pug				×	×					×							×		
Rottweiler	×				×														
Saint Bernard		×			×														
Setter									×			×							
Spaniel		×	×									×				×			
– Cocker spaniel								×	×						×				
Terrier							×		×				×						
– Airedale		×																	
– Fox			×														×		
– Scottish																×			×
– Skye												×							

Disorders of Sight and Hearing

These can be inherited (especially in dogs bred for "harlequin coloring" or blue merle) or acquired (as a secondary effect of distemper).

Impaired Hearing

Loss of hearing must be treated by a veterinarian in good time to prevent total deafness. Deafness has several causes. It develops quite commonly in dogs twelve to fourteen years old, but a serious illness can also affect the hearing of younger dogs. Albinism (a congenital lack of pigments) is often accompanied by deafness.

Inflammation of the Ear

Inflammation of the external ear canal can be caused by an accumulation of ear wax that begins to decay, the presence of foreign bodies, dirt, or water (sometimes from bathing), matted hair inside the ear that interferes with the self-cleaning of the ear canal, and through the closing off of the ear by unkempt drooping ears with long hair. Inflammation of the ears also occurs in cases of infections.
Signs: These are swelling, red skin, increased scaliness, production of sticky to yellowish brown sebum, and ear wax that rots, smells bad, and aggravates the irritation.
Reactions: These are shaking the head, scratching with the feet, rubbing the ears on the floor, tilting the head, and whining with pain. The condition must be treated by a veterinarian.

Allergies and Eczema

These conditions are caused by excessive sensitivity to certain allergens, such as antigenetic proteins, some carbohydrates and fats, and substances derived from some plants, as well as various medications and chemicals.
Signs: These are rashes and reddening or swelling of the skin; in severe cases diarrhea, vomiting, asthma, and sometimes fever are also seen. Eczema usually manifests itself in scaly and itchy skin. If it is acute, there may be inflammations with redness and swelling. In its chronic form it is less dramatic, lingering on with little outward signs of inflammation, but gradually leading to a thickening of the skin. Eczema can turn up on any part of the body, but in large dogs it affects primarily the elbows and the hocks. Spaniels and setters often get it on their lips. Eczema should be treated by a veterinarian. Basically, treatment starts with shaving off all the hair on and around the affected area so that air can get at the skin. Crusty places and bits of hair can be cleaned of gently with a 3% peroxide solution before the eczema is treated according to the veterinarian's directions.

Boils

Boils are pussy inflammations of the hair follicles and the sebaceous glands. Short-haired dogs with deep folds of the skin get them most often, particularly on the nose, chin, and cheeks and on the elbows and hocks.
Treatment: Keep the dog from licking the places by putting a ruff on it. Clean the wound several times a day with 3% hydrogen peroxide or tincture of iodine, and apply a disinfectant salve (such as Betadine) to the surrounding area. If large areas are affected, apply bandages with Domeboro solution and change them every day. Food fortified with vitamins and baker's yeast aids the body's defense reaction. If boils are accompanied by other symp-

toms and fever or if the condition does not clear up, visit the veterinarian.

Lumps and Tumors, Benign and Malignant
Generally speaking, the faster a tumor grows, the greater is the possibility that it is malignant. As dogs grow older, the likelihood of growths increases, just as it does in humans. The most susceptible areas in dogs are the mammary glands, the anal canal, and, in males, the sexual organs. It is up to the veterinarian to decide whether an operation is in order and whether it is likely to be successful.

Paralysis
Partial paralysis is often the consequence of a herniated disk, to which primarily dachshunds and other breeds with long backs and short legs are subject.

In many cases the condition can be cured. If the hindquarters are paralyzed, medications can sometimes, though rarely, bring partial results. Surgery is often more promising. Consult your veterinarian even if the case does not seem serious.

Hip Dysplasia
In some breeds this malformation of the hip joint may be congenital, but it can be aggravated by wrong diet and lead to lameness. Joint deterioration can be diagnosed with the help of x-rays. In a malformed joint, the socket and the ball are flattened and sometimes fit only loosely. If the condition is detected early enough, proper care and food, as well as hormone treatments, can have a beneficial effect and sometimes keep the disorder from progressing past the initial stages.
Prevention: Dogs with hip dysplasia should not be used as breeding stock. (Make sure your puppy's parents are healthy!)

Dislocation of the Kneecap
In lively dogs, and particularly in poodles, this is usually the cause of lameness after a "false step" when jumping or climbing stairs, but the condition can also come on spontaneously. Sometimes the dislocated kneecap moves back in place by itself; if not, the veterinarian must help. In bad cases, an operation is often necessary.

Unprovoked Biting
This is a behavioral disorder that used to occur with some frequency and still does occasionally in unicolored red and black cocker spaniels. The biting is accompanied by signs of rage and fear and can be directed even against the dog's master. In the modern strains of the breed, this disorder has been largely eliminated.

Epileptic Attacks
Epilepsy is sometimes congenital and manifests itself in some breeds when the dog is still young. In other cases it can occur as a result of another illness. The attacks, for which there is usually no external cause, frequently come during the heat period. They usually subside after a few minutes. If the veterinarian diagnoses true epilepsy, it is possible to try to keep the condition under control with medications.

Eclampsia
This is an acute metabolic disorder that affects female dogs, particularly of small and toy breeds. It may occur before or during whelping or even up to five weeks after it.

Signs: These are restlessness, excessive panting, cramps, a panicked look in the eyes, and often a high fever. The condition is life threatening; and it is essential to call the veterinarian promptly.
Preventive measures: Feed your dog vitamin- and mineral-enriched food, especially in the last third of pregnancy, and make sure she gets plenty of exercise while the puppies are nursing.

Twisted Stomach

Dogs of large breeds can suddenly get a twisted stomach if they have been made to play and jump right after having wolfed down a large amount of rich food.
Signs: Restlessness, stomach pains that get worse rapidly, bloating, salivating and panting, retching, and a curiously cautious walk. Only prompt (surgical) treatment by a veterinarian offers any promise of success. if you wait over two hours after the first symptoms, all the efforts to save the animal may be in vain.

Kidney Stones

These may become dangerous, particularly in male dogs.
Signs: These are difficulties in urinating and urine that is cloudy and mixed with blood. The partial and sometimes complete blockage of the urinary tract causes the urine to back up, with painful distension of the bladder and sometimes the kidneys. Mild cases may be alleviated with dietary measures, diuretic medications, and flushing, but often only an operation will help.

Procedures of Handling Every Dog Owner Should Master

To render an animal assistance you must know how to go about it.

Taking the temperature: The normal body temperature of a dog is about 100.6°F (38°C). In very small dogs and in toy breeds it is a little higher, up to 102.5°F (39.0°C). Anything above these temperatures is a fever.

This is how you go about taking the temperature. Insert a thermometer lubricated with some Vaseline in the anus and take it out after about three minutes. It is useful to have the assistance of a second person for holding the dog still (preferably on a table). This person should place one arm around the chest of the dog and hold up the tail with the other.

Weighing a dog: A small dog can simply be set on a bathroom scale. A larger or restless

It is always better to have two people to take a dog's temperature. Lift the dog onto a table. Then, one person holds onto the dog and calms it, while the other lifts up the tail and gently introduces the thermometer into the rectum.

dog must be picked up in your arms. Then, step on the scale with it. By subtracting your weight from the reading of the scale you get the weight of your dog. Very large dogs are best weighed on a luggage scale (at a post office or railroad station). If you ask the official politely and offer to pay a small fee, your request will probably be granted. The average normal weight of adult dogs is mentioned in the descriptions of individual breeds (starting on page 97).

Giving medications in the form of pills or powders: Roll the medication well into a little ball of hamburger and stick it down as far as possible in the dog's throat. Make sure the dog actually swallows it.

Giving drops and larger amounts of liquid: Pull the lip out on one side of the mouth so that a little pouch forms and let the liquid run in slowly. Or, fill the liquid into a plastic syringe that you then (without the needle, of course) insert carefully between the lip and the molars and empty slowly. In both methods, the dog's head should be raised slightly so that the liquid does not run out of the mouth.

Giving a suppository is best accomplished by two people. While one of them holds the dog steady, pets it, and talks to it soothingly, the other introduces the suppository slowly as far into the rectum as possible.

Holding a dog still is essential for a number of treatments. The best way is to hold it so that the head rests in the crook of one arm. This leaves the other hand free to administer the treatment, pet the dog, or provide an extra-secure hold. If the dog is likely to bite, it is better to use a muzzle. In an emergency you can also hold the dog's mouth shut with a loop of bandaging or other material that you tie behind the head.

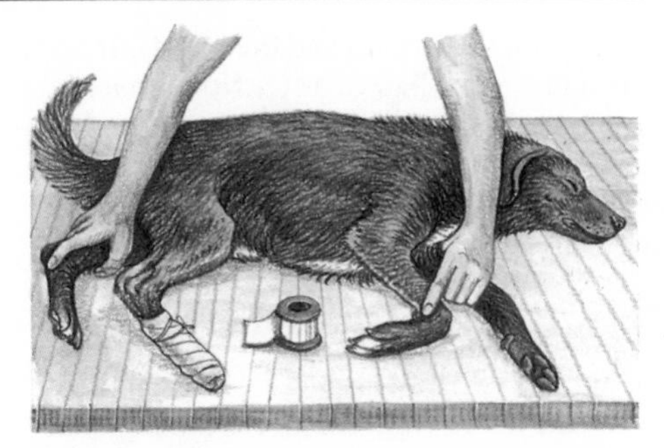

This is how a dog should lie for an examination or for treating wounds. You should always have an assistant when you examine a dog or treat wounds.

First aid requires calmness and a clear head. Try first of all to reassure the injured animal, and try to get it to a veterinarian as quickly as possible (page 82). In case of a serious accident you should telephone ahead so that the veterinarian can get everything ready and start treatment as soon as the dog arrives. Surface wounds should be protected by bandages. Do not use any powders or ointments. Skin abrasions can be treated with a healing salve.

In cases of *internal injuries* or *loss of consciousness,* refrain from force-feeding liquids.

Apply cold compresses to *sprains and bruises* until the swelling begins to go down.

In cases of *poisoning,* induced vomiting can bring relief as long as the poison has not yet entered the bloodstream. Do not feed milk. Instead, give the animal 2 teaspoons of salt dissolved in a little water.

Heavy bleeding can be controlled by placing a tourniquet above the bleeding wound (that is, between the wound and the heart). If no tourniquet is available, any strip of material or a strong rubber band will do, but it should be tight enough to stop the bleeding, and it must be loosened briefly every half hour. Take the dog to the veterinarian as quickly as possible.

First-Aid Kit for Home and Travel

Any household that includes a dog should be equipped with a first-aid kit for the dog that can also be taken along on trips. All medications, salves, powders, and bandaging materials, as well as scissors, tweezers, and a pipette, should be stored where they are handy but safe from children. Get medications for your dog only from your veterinarian, who will be happy to help you decide what you need.

Caution: Do not keep old, deteriorating items and medications past their expiration dates.

The Trip to the Veterinarian

You can use a large, open cardboard box lined with a blanket for taking your dog to the veterinarian. For a dog belonging to a toy breed, a carrying bag left open at the top will also do.

A seriously injured or unconscious dog should be placed on its side on a blanket, which is then picked up like a stretcher. You will, of course, need assistance to do this. To keep an unconscious dog from choking to death, pull its tongue out of its mouth.

Caution: Shock and pain can cause any dog to bite.

Euthanasia

Killing a pet is justified only if the animal is very sick or seriously injured and its future life would be accompanied by constant pain. In such a case euthanasia may be the most humane solution.

This is never true in the case of a pet its owners simply want to be rid of for whatever reason. Even old age accompanied by deteriorating sight and hearing is no justification for having a dog put to sleep. With their keen noses, dogs do not depend on the perfect functioning of eyes and ears to find their way around, and dogs retain their sense of smell into very old age.

If, however, euthanasia seems indicated for one of the reasons just mentioned, then it is our duty to terminate the animal's suffering by a quick death. For this we must take the animal to the veterinarian, so that the end will indeed be painless (through the injection of an anesthetic). All we can do at this point for our friend is to stay with it and reassure it until it has gone to sleep.

Understanding Dogs

Eberhard Trumler, a student of Konrad Lorenz and a well-known authority on dogs, writes in one of his books: "I think that if we want to take dogs seriously we must continue studying their nature just the way we have to continue studying our own nature if we are to take ourselves seriously. . . . Only with the help of well-founded knowledge can we protect dogs from being misused as emotional outlets, merchandise, compensators for complexes, and mere objects to be exhibited at shows."

Anyone who wants to have a dog for egotistical reasons – as a status symbol, for amusement, or to vent repressed feelings on – is unfit to keep a dog and surely is no responsible friend of animals.

To provide a dog with a life worth living and to coexist in happy harmony with it, any potential dog owner should acquire at least a basic understanding of the origin, development, and innate behavior of dogs. Only with this knowledge will you be able to properly understand your pet, its ways of expressing itself, and its needs.

Short History of the Evolution of Dogs

According to the knowledge we have now, it seems probable that there were doglike creatures living in the Americas about 600,000 years ago. Archaeologic finds from much later show that dogs are descended from wolves and were the first domesticated animal. The time of their domestication can be traced back about 12,000 years. The oldest finds, from the Paleolithic – come from a cave in the far northeast of Iraq. The oldest European evidence, discovered in Yorkshire, England, dates more than 9000 years back. A recent excavation in

The wolf, which is the ancestor of all our dogs, belongs to the family Canidae, as do all its relatives shown on this and the following pages.

the Jordan Valley brought further proof of the descent of domestic dogs from wolves. Scientists found a human skeleton 12,000 years old with the bones of the hand resting on the skeletal remains of a wolf or a wolflike dog. This suggests that friendly relations existed between human and dog (or wolf) long before sheep, goats, pigs, or cows were domesticated, that the primitive human separated some wild canine animals from their relatives to train them for use in home (or cave) and on hunts, and that these animals were then bred by humans.

We can easily imagine how this came about. The humans of that time must have run into wild canines in their travels in search of food, and they must occasionally have brought home some pups, at first probably out of the simple desire to vary the menu. In spite of the harsh living conditions of those times, the people must have felt some affection for these young animals. Some pups must have been allowed to grow up, were tamed, and were later taken along to help on hunting expeditions.

Understanding Dogs

Brown hyenas live singly, in pairs, and in family groups. In captivity they have been successfully crossed with domestic dogs.

African wild dogs live in packs whose members help each other. But, in contrast to wolf packs, there is no recognizable ranking order in these packs of wild dogs.

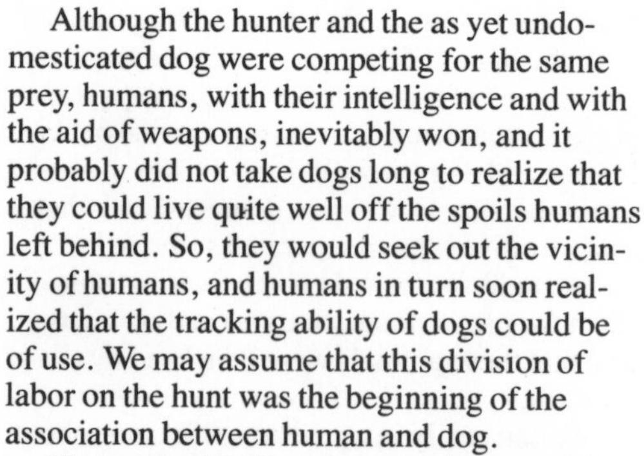

Although the hunter and the as yet undomesticated dog were competing for the same prey, humans, with their intelligence and with the aid of weapons, inevitably won, and it probably did not take dogs long to realize that they could live quite well off the spoils humans left behind. So, they would seek out the vicinity of humans, and humans in turn soon realized that the tracking ability of dogs could be of use. We may assume that this division of labor on the hunt was the beginning of the association between human and dog.

The methods of hunting must have varied with the different kinds of prey, and hunting dogs therefore had to meet different demands. We began to breed them for different qualities by mating animals selected for certain characteristics. This marks the beginning of many of the breeds we know today. In all dogs, even the tamest house dogs, the hunting instinct and original temperament are preserved to a greater or lesser extent. Thanks to their ability to subordinate themselves to people and to adjust to the conditions of coexisting with them, dogs have long since become the best-loved domestic animals.

Despite all the research scientists have done, we cannot yet say with certainty what other animal species, apart from the wolf, contributed to the various breeds of dogs we know today. In back-crossing experiments Professor Wolf Herre performed at the Institute for the Study of Domestic Animals at the University of Kiel, poodles were bred with wolves and jackals. The results indicate clearly that jackals do not belong among the ancestors of dogs. This finding, which runs counter to earlier theories, is based on the evidence of mixed offspring from poodles and jackals, so-called Puschas. These puppies developed atypically compared with their wild ancestors, turning into neurotic, psychically ill-balanced dogs. However, mating of poodles and wolves brought very different results. Although appearance and behavior are not genetically linked, these "Puwos" show that crossings between dogs and wolves can occur in the wild.

In spite of continued changes brought about by the efforts of breeders, our modern dogs still retain wolf characteristics. It is hard to imagine that the tiny chihuahua, standing only about 6 inches (15 centimeters) tall, and the Great Dane, measuring about 32 inches (80 centimeters), have a common ancestor, the same ancestor that all other breeds as well as mongrels go back to, namely, the wolf. Systematic breeding, which has involved both the development of pure strains and the introduction of desired qualities by crossings, has produced the breeds we have today. An ideal stud or dam – a dog that largely conforms to the standard for that breed – should be a dog that combines a superior appearance with excellent character traits. It will also excel in performance and have dominant genes for the most important hereditary factors.

Australian dingoes are domestic dogs gone wild. There are no physical details that distinguish them from regular domestic dogs.

The coyote is the wolfs closest relative. It is found all over North America.

The common or red fox also belongs to the Canidae. It lives in burrows it digs itself, or it takes over abandoned badger dens.

Patterns of Behavior Typical of the Species

Dogs' strongly developed pack instinct shows that they have kept many of their wolflike qualities in spite of their long association with humans. Just as their ancestors used to feel part of their packs, our dogs feel that they belong to their human family. They have the instinctive need to subordinate themselves to the human master in the absence of a pack leader of their own kind. A dog's behavior is not determined solely by instinct; it is also affected by factors in the environment and, as a result of domestication, by the influence of people. In practical terms this means that the less contact with humans a dog has, the more wolflike it will be: the more distrustful of people, defensive of its food, and quick to react aggressively.

The aptitude for learning varies greatly in different breeds and in different individuals, but on the whole it is impressive. The basic patterns are the same for all our dogs; they all make use of the same basic means of expression, which we usually describe as vocal communication and body language.

Vocal Communication

Some dogs bark a lot, and others hardly bark at all; the amount of barking may be a characteristic trait of a particular breed (see Descriptions of Breeds, page 97). However much or little a dog barks, barking is its "language." This language makes use of a broad spectrum of noises, ranging from soft moaning sounds, whining, and growling, to barking proper and the howling that is reminiscent of wolves. Each of these noises also occurs in a number of nuances that the dog uses in certain specific situations. If you listen to your dog attentively, you will gradually learn what each of the different sounds means.

Body Language

Anybody knows that a dog can express pleasure not only by barking but also by wagging its tail. If the dog jumps around happily at the same time, it is pretty obvious that this represents a "ceremony" of friendly greeting. The tail, which, together with the ears, is the most important indicator of mood and conveyor of signals, generally expresses the following feelings:

Tail extended horizontally indicates a sense of contentment.

Tail sticking up signals increased attentiveness or excitement.

Tail carried low between the legs is a sign of reserve or fear.

Depending on the dog's breed and the length of the tail, these signals are not always reliable or easy to read. In the case of purebred greyhounds or whippets, for instance, one cannot go by this barometer of mood because these dogs almost always keep their tails between their legs except when they are running.

A dog sprawled out flat on the floor is not necessarily suffering from heat or exhaustion. This posture can also be an expression of well-being and contentment. An alert, tense posture when standing can mean two things: Either the dog is full of excited anticipation, in which case it will wag its tail, or if the tail is still and the hair on the neck rises up, it is extremely nervous and about to explode in a fit of anger.

Facial Expressions and Gestures

It is not quite as simple to interpret a dog's facial expressions. Elements of facial expression are wrinkling the nose, blinking the eyes, raising the upper lip (sometimes giving the impression of a grin), and bending or folding down the ears. Expressions that could be read clearly in the face of the dog's ancestor, the wolf, are hidden in many breeds behind a thick

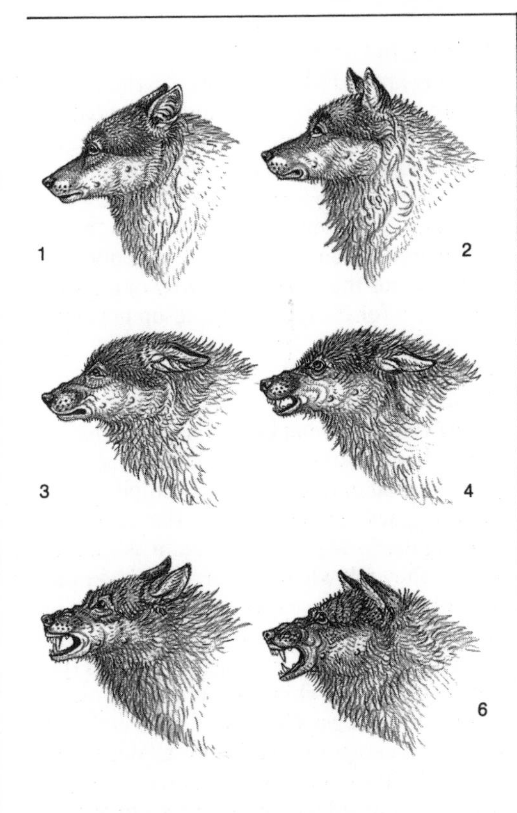

Facial expressions of a dog, shown as they look in a wolf.
1. Peacefulness and relaxation.
2. Attention, interest: The ears are pricked up.
3. Uncertainty, fear: The ears are flattened, the lips raised a little. Flight or attack are equally likely.
4. Fear and rising anger: The ears are completely flat, and the lips raised.
5. Readiness for attack: The ears are rising, the lips drawn way back.
6. About to attack: The ears point forward, and the muzzle is open.

curtain of hair. Yorkshire terriers, Maltese, Old English sheepdogs, and Komondors are examples here.

Generally speaking, the ears give the best clues to the dog's moods. In a dog with naturally erect ears,

Raised (or *pricked*) ears mean self-confidence, attentiveness, readiness to guard;

Ears pointed in a certain direction mean that the dog has heard some interesting sounds from that direction, sounds that are attracting its attention;

Ears lying flat either sideways or pointing back demonstrate uncertainty or a skeptical attitude and—if accompanied by growling and fur standing up—aggression.

It is more difficult to read these signals in a dog with floppy ears.

An attempt to raise the ears as straight as possible shows heightened attentiveness or an effort to localize especially interesting sounds.

Ears hanging down loosely signal indifference and a normal, relaxed frame of mind.

To express love and gratitude, the tongue, too, is used as a means of communication. When our dog wants to lick us—which we should not permit for hygienic reasons—it is making a *gesture of affection* that it has inherited from its ancestors. "Shaking hands" is nothing more than an elaboration of the "kneading" (pushing rhythmically against the mother's teats with the paws) a puppy does to stimulate the flow of milk. In grown dogs, this gesture develops into a *begging gesture.*

A dog that jumps up on you in its happiness is performing a *greeting ritual* from its "wild past." This is how wolf parents bringing home prey were received by their pups. If you want to break your dog of this habit you should never do it by some brutal method, such as stepping on its hind toes. After all, it is not being bad but simply acting in accordance with inborn behavior patterns. There are better ways of achieving your goals. Evade the jumping puppy, and if necessary, say "no" firmly every time it jumps. You must remain consistent and never permit the animal to jump up on you, not even in play.

Digging and Burying

The burying of bones and leftover meat is also a carryover from the dog's wolf past and was originally done to store food and let meat cure. Often the survival of the wild animals depended on these food reserves hidden in the ground. Although our canine housemates are unlikely to experience famine, they have been unable to shed this habit, which has become part of their flesh and blood. They continue to bury not only food they cannot manage to eat at the time, but also toys. When they do this, they neatly push the dug-up earth back over the hole. Some dogs always remember precisely where they buried something. Others get sloppy and forget all about their buried treasures because fresh food always keeps turning up.

The habit some dogs have of scratching or digging on the hard living-room floor is more likely to spring from the urge to create a comfortable sleeping hole. The same behavior can be observed in a dog that is about to go to sleep in its basket and first scratches to arrange a nice hollow to settle into. This behavior, too, goes back to old times and still survives even though living conditions have changed dramatically for dogs in the process of living with humans.

Turning in Circles

Turning around several times in a tight circle before lying down and curling up in a ball is another habit that dates back to the ancient past. The dog's wild ancestors had to stamp down the grass to form a nestlike hollow before they could settle down in it. This "gymnastic" exercise seems to serve another purpose as well: It aids the extreme curving of the spine necessary for the typical curled-up posture of a sleeping dog.

Scent Marks

A dog finds out what is new in the world through its nose; with it the dog "reads" the markings other dogs have left behind on tree trunks, gates, and lamp posts. For a male dog, leaving marks is just as important as examining them: they tell where his territorial boundaries are. Male dogs raise their legs not just for the purpose of emptying their bladders but much more frequently for leaving scent marks (tiny sprays of urine), which also obliterate marks left by other dogs. This leaving and collecting of scent messages is crucial for all dogs but especially for males. Be sure, therefore, to give your dog all the time he needs to decipher and place his scent messages in peace. There is so much else of his natural behavior that he has had to give up to coexist with humans!

Female dogs are not quite as intent on leaving and reading scent messages. Only shortly before and during their heat period do they show an increased interest in the markings of male dogs. They do not claim a territory of their own and therefore do not have to mark its boundaries. That is why they urinate only to relieve themselves and squat to do so, which means that a walk with a female dog is much less punctuated by pauses than a walk with a mal

Necessary Contact with Others of Their Kind

People who live in seclusion and avoid all contact with the world around them are to be pitied because they miss out on the experience of getting to know others and finding out what others are like, how they live, and what they think. They grow more and more insecure and usually turn into shy hermits or curious eccentrics. The same thing happens to a dog whose overly anxious master or mistress keeps it from meeting with other dogs. Since these unfortunate creatures have no experience in dealing with others of their kind, they react with fear, shyness, irritation, or aggression when they do happen to come in contact with another dog. Their anxiety turns them into nervous, yapping wrecks or makes them bite out of sheer fear. Dogs are by nature social pack animals for whom communication with others of their kind is a basic need.

For your dog to become familiar with the age-old dog rituals, you should let your puppy meet other dogs as often as possible. At these occasions it will learn not only how to behave like a proper dog but will also learn how it fits into the social hierarchy (see The Third and Fourth Months: The Phase of Establishing Rank Order, page 93).

When two dogs that are not acquainted with each other meet, the first thing they do is touch noses. This preliminary testing, which always occurs between healthy dogs, determines right away whether the dogs are going to like each other. The next step is a mutual sniffing of the rear end. To provide a more complete picture, a leg is raised now and then so that the "stranger" can get acquainted with the special scent of the other and memorize it. In the course of the rituals it will become apparent quickly whether friendship or enmity is likely to develop or whether the two are completely disinterested in each other.

Checking out each other's anal region is the next step in getting acquainted after the dogs have sniffed noses.

Fighting for Rank

Basically, meetings between dogs resemble those between people. If dogs like each other, they wag their tails just as people shake hands. If they cannot stand each other they – again, just like people – avoid each other or growl (or mutter) something at each other; if worse comes to worst there is a fight. But there is one big difference between human and canine meetings: In dogs, the ranking order (social hierarchy) plays a crucial role. To determine which dog ranks above the other, an anal check is necessary, and if there is any doubt in the matter, a fight ensues to settle it. The scenario runs something like this: Two dogs stand facing each other, growling softly, tails held stiff, and lips raised. This means that a state of "highest emergency" has been reached. If the hair on the nape of the neck, the back, and the root of the tail is raised now, it is clear that only a physical contest can settle which of the two animals is the stronger, that is, ranks above the other. This battle, which is accompanied by fierce growling, usually looks worse than it really is. The growling and snarling are meant more to intimidate the opponent and demoralize it, and as a rule the louder the noise level, the smaller the likelihood of real danger.

Nature has built in a safety mechanism to prevent fights from getting out of hand. As soon as one of the contestants realizes that it is weaker than the other, it lies on its back and exposes its vulnerable throat. This gesture (at least in the case of normal dogs) has an effect similar to that of raising a white flag as a sign of capitulation. If the victor tries to put its jaws around the defenseless throat, an inhibiting instinct takes over, and the duel is over.

Gesture of subordination: In a battle to determine rank order, the weaker dog rolls on its back, exposing its defenseless throat to the opponent. This gesture always spells the end of the fight.

As I have already said, these behavioral patterns that are so important for the survival of the species function as described in all normal dogs. Overbred dogs or those that have been improperly treated and have consequently become behaviorally disturbed do not obey these natural rules and sometimes bite even puppies, something no normal dog would dream of doing.

Dogs that always walk on a leash feel twice as strong as they are because of this tangible contact with their master and therefore initiate fights much more often than dogs that are allowed to run free and are used to encounters with other dogs.

It is better not to try to separate two fighting dogs, or you may well wind up being the main casualty. If you step in, not only the strange dog but also your own may well bite you in the heat of battle. A forceful separation of the two four-footed contestants intent on battling each other can be accomplished only if their owners act quickly and at the same time, each grabbing the hind legs of their own dog, lifting it up, and thus breaking up the fight. If this maneuver is successful, peace is usually restored quickly because most dogs are relieved not to have to fight to the bitter end.

If bravery does not appeal to you, you may succeed with a diversionary tactic. This should be applied before the encounter threatens to deteriorate into earnest fighting. Call out a command the dog usually responds to enthusiastically. This gives it a chance to retreat in time and without losing face. Be sure to minimize the use of such fake commands, or you will undermine the trustful relationship between yourself and your dog. Let me stress once again that the more chance a dog gets to meet with other dogs the more secure it will be in its behavior toward them.

Display Behavior

In ethology, that is, the study of animal behavior, the term "display behavior" can apply to ways in which dogs set up ranking orders as well as to other aspects of canine behavior. Here, display means bragging, showing off, pretending to be bigger than life, raising the hair, showing the teeth, and growling, all of which are done to cow an opponent, make it feel insecure, demoralize it, and make it retreat. When it is all over, the dog that has exaggerated most convincingly is the winner. In this way the question of which contestant is the stronger and therefore should rank above the other is often settled without resort to actual fighting.

The Sensory Organs of Dogs

Smell and Taste

The excellent sense of smell, surpassing that of most other mammals, permits a dog to orient itself primarily with its nose, its most highly developed sensory organ. With the help of its very mobile and always moist nose, a dog can smell substances in extremely small concentrations, such as human sweat diluted a million times. Specially trained dogs, such as those used by customs officials to detect narcotics, can even "filter out" individual smells from a mixture of several scents. Search dogs that are used to find victims buried in avalanches can even smell people lying under 5 meters of snow.

The sense of taste, which is also well-developed in dogs, is closely associated with their extremely acute sense of smell.

Sight and Hearing

Dogs are naturally farsighted, and their vision is primarily organized to register movements. Although their field of vision is greater than that of humans, their three-dimensional vision is quite limited. Dogs were at one point nocturnally active animals and therefore have a reflective layer at the back of the eyes, which allows them to see somewhat better in dim light than humans can. Visual acuity varies from dog to dog. Greyhounds and whippets, for instance, have considerably better vision

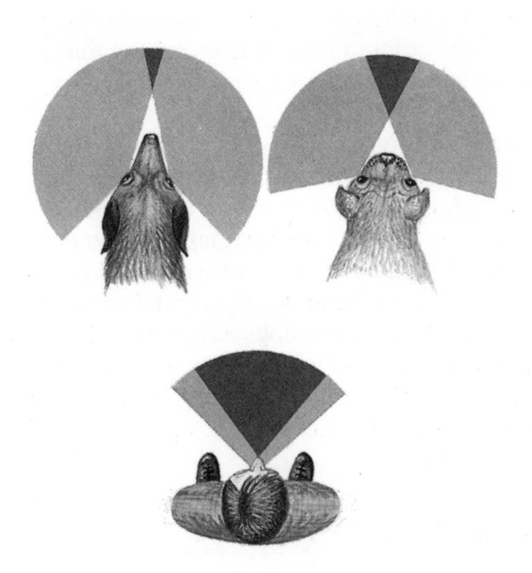

Field of vision of humans and dogs: Depending on the shape of the skull and the placement of the eyes, a dog's angle of vision is between 270 and 200 degrees. In humans it is only about 100 degrees.

than members of other breeds: The great speeds they achieve when following a trail would be impossible with the nose on the ground.

A dog's ears are capable of hearing sounds that are inaudible to us. The human ear registers sounds from about 16,000 to 20,000 Hertz (sound waves per second), but a dog perceives sounds from about 70 to 100,000 Hertz. That is why a trained hunting dog will respond to commands from a so-called soundless dog whistle (in the supersonic range of about 30,000 Hertz) at distances up to 500 yards. The sounds of the whistle are inaudible to both hunter and game. Their excellent hearing also explains why many dogs make such good watchdogs. Their ability to pick out specific sounds (such as the hum of their owner's car) with incredible accuracy from among many similar sounds is also impressive.

Sense of Touch

The network of nerves that extends over the entire body of the dog serves, among other things, to register tactile stimuli and temperature. The most sensitive areas are the front of the nose, the tongue, the lips, and the pads on the feet. In addition, dogs have especially modified hairs, or whiskers, that are extremely sensitive. They are lodged deep in the skin and are located primarily near the lips and in the eyebrows.

From Puppy to Adult Dog

The First Two Weeks: The Vegetative Phase

Puppies begin to search for their mother's teats as soon as they are born. Since their eyes and ears are still closed and even their sense of smell is still almost nonexistent, they must rely on their tactile sense to find the all-important source of milk. An innate behavior pattern of crawling around in circles also aids them in this. The head and body are too large in proportion to the paws, and it is not easy for the baby dogs to control their movements. When they find their mother they shove their heads along her fur until they reach a teat, and then they suck until they sink back sated and exhausted. To sleep, they snuggle up closely to their littermates, and in the warmth thus generated they stay comfortable for a while, even if the mother leaves them for a bit. In this phase they are not yet interested in social contact; they follow only the bare law of survival: "Each for itself!" Keeping the puppies clean is completely up to the mother because all the little creatures are capable of at this point are eating and sleeping.

The Third Week: The Transitional Phase

Although the eyes and ears open toward the end of the second week, the ability to see and hear does not really develop until about the eighteenth day. The sensitivity to smell is also only in its beginning stages. Although there is still no social interaction, one does observe certain reactions and some desire to take in the world. The puppies now begin to leave the box occasionally to follow their mother. The discovery of a new world with all its unknown obstacles and dangers begins. At first the puppies, which are still quite clumsy, use gestures of subordination to deal with insurmountable obstacles. A tiny puppy, for instance, that feels bothered by the nosing curiosity of an older dog, will simply drop on its back. This reaction of exposing its throat to the superior animal is at this stage a purely instinctual and therefore unconscious action. In a grown dog it has the function of inhibiting aggression (page 90).

The Fourth to the Seventh Week: The Imprinting Phase

During this period the puppy gains in security; its movements become surer and quicker; and its ability to understand develops. It begins to discover itself, others of its kind, the world around it, and people. It learns to master its voice and to express its states of mind by using voice and tail. In play with siblings, social interaction ranging from gestures of affection to threatening behavior, is first practiced. Frequent contact, especially physical contact, with its human caretaker leaves impressions on the puppy that will affect its relationship with people for the rest of its life. If the human is accepted like another member of its own kind, this connection can develop into permanent friendship. This imprinting phase is crucial for the young dog because what it does not learn at this stage can be made up for later on only with great difficulty, if at all, but what it learns at this point stays with it for life.

The Eighth to the Twelfth Week: The Socializing Phase

It is during this phase that puppies learn to distinguish between fun and seriousness in their interaction with their own kind as well as with humans. Their eagerness for learning is boundless as long as learning is like a game. The dog parents seem to be aware of this because they now start to teach the puppies what they need to know and cleverly make use of their playfulness in doing so. The littermates also learn from each other: how to fight, how to capitulate, how to defend oneself, how to get one's way, and how to get reconciled. Ferocious tussles take place with much growling, biting, fleeing, and chasing. Each puppy tests just how far it can go and learns to know its own strength in the process, how to use this strength to best advantage, and how to control it.

This phase of development, that is, between eight and twelve weeks, is the best time for you to get your new puppy because this is when the foundation of a strong social bond between the dog and its master should be laid. Now, at the latest, the basic training (see Basic Dog Obedience, page 45) is begun. At this point the puppy is still eager to learn, adaptable, and malleable, and it can be shaped into an obedient and sympathetic friend for life. The first lessons should not be too demanding. They should evolve out of play and be wisely paced.

The Third and Fourth Months: The Phase of Establishing Rank Order

The puppies continue to grow in body, mind, and spirit; their play becomes more "grown-up" because they know that to defend their rights they need to use not only their physical strength but also their intelligence. They have learned to subordinate themselves to a dominant animal, whether this animal is physically more powerful or mentally superior. The willingness and need to accept a "lead dog" (or a human master as a substitute) becomes more and more obvious.

This is the time when young dogs should get as much experience as possible outside the house, too, experience that will also leave its mark on the dog for the rest of its life. By encountering other dogs the young animal can familiarize itself with the etiquette that dominates the social life of dogs. Knowing these rules enhances and strengthens the dog's self-confidence. A dog that rarely practices these rules is likely to behave inappropriately in later encounters since it never had a chance to learn better. It may resort to acts of aggression that may have dire consequences for it. At this stage it is not yet grown up, and since it still has its "baby smell," it enjoys special protection. You therefore need not worry as a rule if a strange dog runs up to your puppy, and there is no cause for alarm even if the stranger gives it a shove with its nose to teach the puppy its place or growls at it. This is true for all adult dogs, assuming that they are normal, that is, psychologically well-adjusted. Since behaviorally disturbed dogs do exist, it is best to watch the strange dog carefully at first. Nevertheless, undue concern is not called for since such abnormal dogs are in a minute minority. You yourself would be contributing to a neurotic development of your dog if, out of sheer anxiety, you kept it from all contact with others of its species. So let it get acquainted with as many other dogs as possible so that it can learn to grasp the rules that govern social intercourse and learn to behave in accordance with its place in the ranking order.

Now you should start training your dog to subordinate its will to yours. Practice the commands "come," "sit," and "stay." Do this at first in the context of play, and do not overdo it or your dog will lose its enjoyment of learning.

The Fifth and Sixth Months: The Phase of Learning to Fit into the Pack

This is the time when packs of wolves or wild dogs start taking the younger members along on the hunt to teach them how to catch prey and how to overcome any difficulties and dangers arising from this pursuit. Only a team that works together reliably, one in which the duties of each member are clearly defined by its rank, can hunt together successfully. The alpha animal, the strongest and smartest animal, is in charge of the pack. For all the rest of the pack, subordination is the law. This alone makes survival possible.

At this stage of development, the hunting instinct awakens in our domestic dogs, too, and with it the predilection for outings on their own. This is why we should keep them busy now, teaching them to fetch, for instance, which they should learn as a game. You must spend a lot of time with your dog at this point because it must develop enough trust in you to accept you as its "pack leader." This will not happen unless, as I have mentioned before, you are consistent in your educational efforts. You must punish any instance of disobedience immediately, just the way the lead wolf would. If you do so matter-of-factly without getting excited and are also generous with praise, you will find that you have a willing and eager student.

Now is also the time to introduce your dog to all the dangers and other aspects of the wider environment. Get it used to the noise and confusion of city traffic (keeping it on the leash, of course), as well as to encounters with other kinds of animals in the countryside. Make sure it still gets plenty of play time, but gradually teach it discipline.

From the Seventh Month: The Phase of Puberty

Most dogs reach sexual maturity at eight or nine months of age. Others, depending on breed and size, may reach it either earlier or later. You know that a male dog has reached adulthood when he lifts his leg to urinate. With female dogs, which mature sexually somewhat earlier than males, you know when they enter their first heat period and suddenly show an interest in male dogs. If you do not watch out, your female dog might conceive at this stage, but it is better not to mate her until her second heat (page 39).

Along with sexual maturity comes a phase of adolescent rebelliousness. The dog becomes wild and obstinate, trying to shed its painstakingly acquired training and being deliberately disobedient. It behaves just like a young rowdy that, as it grows in physical strength, acts up and challenges established power. Now you must be especially strict so that all your previous efforts do not come to naught. Be even more on the lookout than before not to let your pupil get away with anything. If it senses even the slightest chance of asserting its will against yours, it will try it, hoping ultimately to become top dog. If it succeeds it will try to call all the shots and tyrannize the whole family. Your influence will have shrunk to practically nil. Do not let things get to that point. Be as strict as necessary, but keep in mind that this is a difficult time for the dog as well. It must define its own identity and find its place in the world. That is why you must treat it during this puberty period with consistent strictness and at the same time with extra love.

When your dog is fully mature (small breeds after about one year, large ones often not until they are two years old), it will settle down. Its temperament will be more stable, and it will develop into a reliable, obedient partner that behaves in all situations in accordance with its status as a dog. Now it is also ready for training as a working or utility dog (page 51).

If a dog does not follow this pattern of development, if it is unpredictable and disobedient, its master alone is to blame. Its master has failed as an educator. As I have said before, everyone gets the dog they deserve. Dogs that live an existence devoid of challenge and occupation, that are kept in a manner that runs counter to their nature, that receive hardly any training, are improperly fed, or spoiled—these dogs atrophy psychologically and physically. This is true cruelty to animals.

Behaviorally Disturbed Dogs

Unfortunately, not all dogs are "normal." There are some with character defects that can be due either to genetic factors or to improper handling during their growing phase. Just what does "normal" or "disturbed" mean when applied to dogs?

A healthy dog has a stable, well-balanced, even nature or character. This quality is a prerequisite for a dog that is to be used for breeding purposes or for work. "Nature" and "character" are collective terms used to describe the sum total of traits that are partially inherited and partially acquired. A dog with a "good nature" is physically and mentally healthy and resistant. It is courageous, steady, and self-confident. It behaves under all circumstances in keeping with what it is. This is to say, it always reacts in accordance with the patterns of canine behavior that are deeply rooted in its subconscious, as well as with the principles it has absorbed through experience and education. By treating and training a puppy in a manner appropriate to its stage, we can have a positive effect on the later character of the dog.

Character disorders in a dog can be caused by hereditary factors but are more often due to negative environmental influences and to wrong training during puppyhood. The resulting maladjustment can manifest itself in various ways, but usually in the form of "overreacting." Typical manifestations are excessive aggressiveness; oversensitivity, especially to sounds; exaggerated timidity; irritability; and destructiveness. Such behavior that deviates from the norm can stem from a number of causes.

- *Poor selection for breeding.* The reason for this is usually an overemphasis on physical beauty and perfection at the expense of keeping the stock healthy and furthering the best character traits.
- *A serious disease* (such as canine distemper or leptospirosis) that leaves behind irreparable brain damage.
- *Misguided education and inappropriate handling.* This is often the result of sheer ignorance but still should be attributed to lack of concern for the animal. Another prime cause is the apparently ineradicable tendency to "humanize" animals. When applied to dogs with their wolflike heritage, this is an especially grievous error. This kind of affection, no matter how well-intentioned, reveals a total misunderstanding of love for animals.
- *Being ignored and deprived of activity.* This can lead to a buildup of instinctual energy that erupts in aggressive actions. The best and most natural way for the dog to work off accumulated aggression is to get plenty of exercise in the fresh air, preferably combined with play and learning.

All this goes to show that not only the dog's background and the conditions under which it lives, but also strict and consistent training and proper handling, affect its psychic well-being.

If you purchase your dog not from a kennel that mass-produces dogs but from a recognized and experienced breeder and raise it in accordance with the principles and rules recommended in this book, you may be confident that it will develop into a healthy and normal dog.

Descriptions of Dog Breeds

Large Dogs

Afghan Hound

Photos, pages 10 and 20

Height (at withers)/Weight: Males: 27 inches, plus or minus 1 inch; about 60 pounds. Females: 25 inches, plus or minus 1 inch; about 50 pounds.
Color: White, black, gray-brown, rust, or tan; either unicolored or a combination of two or three colors; white markings, especially on the head, are not desirable.
Suitable: People who enjoy having a large, beautiful, and conspicuous dog and who might consider dog racing.
Less Suitable: Conservative folk and people who are not willing to pay tribute to the animal's beauty by devoting time and energy every day to grooming the dog's coat.
Needs: A large apartment or a house with a yard, and sensitive yet rigorous training. Afghans need to be carefully brushed and combed every day and thoroughly cleaned and rubbed dry if they get wet. They need to get plenty of exercise no matter what the weather and to run free as much as possible.
Good points: A dignified and majestic appearance. Afghans are hardy, tough, sensitive, intelligent, and very affectionate. They rarely bark; they are suspicious of strangers but never vicious. They thrive in any climate. Afghans can run as fast as 28 miles per hour (45 kilometers per hour).
Drawbacks: If improperly treated or trained too rigidly, Afghans can become timid, distrustful, and nervous. Regular grooming is absolutely essential and requires considerable time.
Life Expectancy: Ten to fifteen years.

Borzoi

Photo, back cover

Height/Weight: Mature male should be at least 28 inches, and mature female at least 26 inches at the withers. Range in weight for males from 75 to 105 pounds and for females from 15 to 20 pounds less.
Color: Any solid color from white through shades of gold, red, and gray to black; often piebald (that is, irregular white patches) in any of the colors mentioned.
Suitable: People who live in the country and have plenty of space and time for this large, decorative dog with its great need for exercise.
Less Suitable: City and indoors people and small apartments.
Needs: Adequate freedom of movement. Is best kept in a house or, if that is impossible, in a large apartment and with access to a yard. A borzoi needs a long daily outing, perhaps running along beside a horseback or bicycle rider. Its elegant coat requires regular care (daily combing and brushing), which need not take much time, however. A good teacher is essential.
Good Points: Sensitive, intelligent, eager to learn, and very faithful. Indoors, a borzoi is quiet and reserved, but outside it is active, spirited, and loves to run, achieving top speeds of up to 30 miles per hour (50 kilometers per hour). Information on organized dog races can be obtained from the Borzoi Club of America (address, page 000). Borzois bark only rarely.
Drawbacks: A poorly trained, disobedient borzoi will run deer and other wild creatures if it roams free and if its hunting instinct is awakened by the scent of game.
Life Expectancy: Ten to fourteen years.
Consider Before You Buy: Training a borzoi, especially a male borzoi, can be problematic; it requires a lot of kind understanding for the animal but at the same time strict consistency. Rigorous, forced "drilling" achieves nothing and can even result in the opposite of a good education.

French Mastiff

Drawing next page

Dogge de bordeaux

Height/Weight: Males: minimum 30 inches at the shoulder; to 185 pounds. Females: minimum 27.5 inches at the shoulder; to 175 pounds.

The French mastiff is loyal and gentle but looks rather intimidating with its grim expression and powerful body.

Color: Mahogany red in various shades, also with a dark face, the darker the better and always darker than the body.
Suitable. People who want the protection of a dog that commands respect.
Less Suitable. Small apartments and older, physically not very strong, or timid persons. The French Mastiff is not a farm dog and should not be kept exclusively outdoors.
Needs: At least a fair-sized apartment with access to a yard, although it needs relatively little exercise. To train it, it should have a kind master with experience in handling dogs. The care of its coat is not demanding.
Good Points: Sensitive, therefore easily hurt, but does not bear grudges; lovable and devoted. Its fierce appearance alone will scare away troublemakers. It is powerful, robust, and very brave, and will attack in earnest if there is real sign of danger.
Drawbacks: Its education can be problematic. If it gets in the hands of the wrong person, it can develop into an aggressive and vicious dog.
Life Expectancy: About ten years.

Great Dane

Photo, page 19

Height/Weight: Males should not be less than 30 inches at the shoulders, but it is preferable that they are 32 inches or more, providing they are well proportioned to their height; females should not be less than 28 inches at the shoulders, but it is preferable that they are 30 inches or more, providing they are well proportioned for their height. Males to 150 pounds; females to 135 pounds.
Color: Glossy black; light to golden yellow with a black face; golden yellow with strong black cross stripes; also harlequin (pure white with irregular black patches distributed all over the body).
Suitable: Only for people with a real affinity for dogs. Training is not easy and requires empathy and understanding.
Less Suitable: The average person, especially anyone who finds it difficult to train even a dachshund.
Needs: Preferably a house with a large yard because this dog requires exercise and things to keep it busy. It must be trained strictly but not with harshness, and thus should have a firm but loving teacher. Grooming is relatively simple.
Good Points: An elegant, proud, intelligent, and very strong dog. Makes a courageous, reliable guard and watchdog (suited for training as a work dog) that will turn aggressive only if circumstances dictate it or, especially, if its master is threatened. Strangers automatically respect it because of its sheer appearance. Is fond of children.
Drawbacks: If a Great Dane is not raised properly it may try to become boss in the family and tyrannize everybody or, worse yet, get completely out of its master's control and turn extremely vicious and dangerous.
Life Expectancy: About twelve years.

Hovawart

Photo, page 19

Height/Weight: Male: 24 to 28 inches; 66 to 88 pounds. Female: 22 to 26 inches; 55 to 77 pounds.
Color: Black, dark blond, and black with tan areas.

The English springer spaniel is one of the oldest English trailing dogs.

Suitable: A guard dog on a farm, as its name, which means "warden of the estate and farmyard," suggests. It also makes a good family dog. Not known in the United States. The breed disappeared during the nineteenth century, but was revived by German breeders in the early 1900s.
Less Suitable: People who like to leave decisions up to others and do not like the idea of spending a lot of time doing things with their dog.
Needs: A large apartment or house with a yard or, better yet, a homestead it can guard and protect. Its coat must be groomed every day, but not very extensively. Needs a person experienced with dogs to train it or work with it. Suited for training as a utility dog.
Good Points: A very reliable guard dog and protector that also likes to baby-sit children. Obedient, smart, and trustworthy. Can be kept in a run. Devoted and loyal to a master whose authority it senses and acknowledges.
Drawbacks: Incorrect or inconsistent training and a lack of activity can lead to a buildup of aggression. Hovawarts are relatively slow to mature and should not be trained for work – if that is what they are meant for – until they are three to four years old.
Life Expectancy: Twelve to fourteen years.

Irish Wolfhound

Photo, page 19

Height/Weight: Male: 32 to about 36 inches; 120 pounds and more; Female: no less than 30 inches; 90 pounds and more.
Color: Pure white, red, fawn, gray, black, and – found most commonly – brindle, or any other color that appears in the deerhound.
Suitable: Owners of homes and estates of generous proportions and people who live in a grand style and wish to have an imposing, watchful, but good-natured housemate and walking companion.
Less Suitable: Most normal mortals living average lives in average living quarters. Not recommended for newcomers to dogdom.
Needs: Lots of space and freedom of movement. Should spend as much time as possible in the fresh air, the yard, for instance, and still have a daily walk with its master when there is some opportunity to run free. Thorough grooming required but is not very time-consuming: brush and comb daily and curry once or twice a week. An Irish wolfhound needs a kind and understanding master who treats it with strict consistency but never harshly.
Good Points: This giant among dogs is gentle and patient, especially with children, and is very affectionate, primarily toward its master. It is very even-tempered.
Drawbacks: There are some problems transporting a dog of this size, for instance in a passenger car. Improper training and needless egging can turn it dangerously aggressive.
Life Expectancy: About twelve years.

Neapolitan or Italian Mastiff

Photo, page 19

Height/Weight: Male, 26 to 30 inches; female, 24 to 28 inches. All, up to 154 pounds.
Color: Black, gray, lead color, yellow; all shades of gray, brindled; also, all colors can be combined with white markings on the chest and on the toes.
Suitable: Strong and energetic people who can take proper charge of this "powerhouse" of a dog.
Less Suitable: People who are inexperienced in raising and training large dogs and for physically delicate or older people.
Needs: A strong hand and absolute consistency in training. This mastiff is best kept in a run but should not be totally excluded from family activities. It should be taken for a good walk every day. The

Terriers:
Above left: Airedale terrier; above right: Scottish terrier.
Center left: Smooth fox terrier; center right: bullterrier.
Below left: Yorkshire terrier; below right: Skye terrier.

care of the coat is unproblematic, but the cost of keeping such a dog in food – it should get plenty of meat – is considerable.
Good Points: Its ferocious exterior is intimidating, but this dog is basically a sweet, affectionate creature with a calm temperament. It gets very attached to the family and especially to its master and, if trained for this purpose, makes an excellent watch and guard dog.
Drawbacks: A Neapolitan mastiff usually has patience only with the children of its own family. Because of its power and size alone, it is not suitable for being with children. If badly raised it can be unpredictable, dangerously aggressive, and may tend to bite.
Life Expectancy: About ten years.

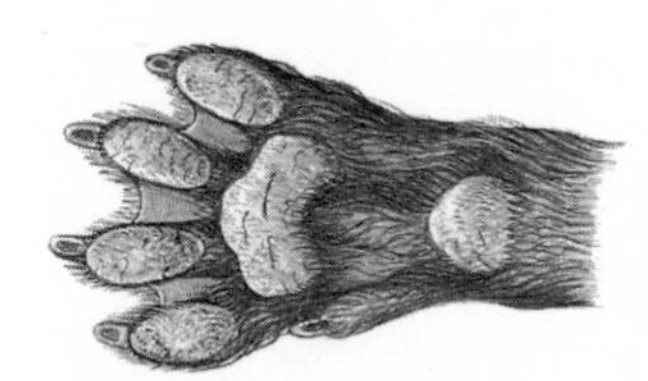

The feet of a Newfoundland are webbed. When these dogs swim, they extend the toes so that the skin between them is fully exposed.

Newfoundland

Photo, page 19

Height/Weight: Male: 27 to 30 inches; 150 pounds; Females 24.5 to 27.5 inches; 120 pounds.
Color: Black (sometimes with a blue or an auburn sheen), brown, and bronze.
Suitable: Farmsteads or country inns, especially if there is a lake nearby.
Less Suitable: Keeping in the city. This is no apartment dog!
Needs: Lots of room. Does not mind being kept in a run as long as it is taken for walks often enough. It should be outdoors as much as possible. Its coat needs frequent combing, brushing, and currying.
Good Points: Very alert, courageous, docile, and loyal. A Newfoundland is a large, strong, and robust dog that loves to swim and is good-natured and long-suffering even with children.
Drawbacks: If it is left by itself too much, it tends to become inactive and lazy and prone to illness. If it is kept indoors all the time it loses the undercoat and sheds a lot.
Life Expectancy: Ten years.

Saint Bernard

Photos, page 9 and back cover

Short-haired and long-haired

Height/Weight: Male: no less than 27.5 inches: female: no less than 25.5 inches: 120 to 165 pounds. The female is of finer and more delicate build.
Color: White with red or red with white; the red can be of different shades; often with a black face and a regular white blaze.
Suitable: People who do things on a grand scale. Best kept by owners of country inns, rich farmers, and hermits who already have experience with dogs.
Less Suitable: The average person and especially the physically and psychologically delicate.
Needs: Lots of room and plenty to eat. The owner should have a friend at the butcher's shop or else plenty of cash for the considerable costs of providing enough food. This is no dog for apartments or the city. A Saint Bernard should be kept in a well-equipped run, and it needs a long daily walk even if it spends most of its time outdoors.
Good Points: A Saint Bernard makes a very good watchdog without barking a lot. It is faithful, obedient, good-natured, placid, and gets along well with children. Excellent rescue dog (if trained), especially for finding people lost in the mountains.
Drawbacks: Often has a marked antipathy for small dogs. Some excessively heavy Saint Bernards become lazy and sedentary and consequently prone to illness. The fur of long-haired types must be brushed and combed more often and more thoroughly than that of the short-haired ones.
Life Expectancy: About 10 years.

Saluki

Photo, page 20

Height/Weight: Male: 23 to 28 inches; to 60 pounds. Female: at least 21 inches; to 55 pounds.
Color: Gray, cream, golden, fox red, fawn; any of these colors combined with sandy yellow or brown; white with sandy yellow or auburn markings; black with white, sandy yellow, or auburn markings; tricolors may be white, black, and red or white, black, and sandy yellow.
Suitable: People who would like an extremely swift and graceful dog that can also be used for racing.
Less Suitable: Stay-at-homes who are not fond of outdoor activities.
Needs: Its own place in a large apartment and enough daily exercise outdoors. The length of the outing is not so crucial. What does matter is that the dog be able to run free, accompanying you on a bicycle ride, for instance.
Good Points: Relatively easy to take care of. Sensitive, affectionate, very eager for action. Excellent candidate for dog racing (information from Saluki Club of America, address, page 134). Racing speed, about 30 to 33 miles per hour (50 to 55 kilometers per hour).
Drawbacks: Although not really refractory, the Saluki finds it difficult to subordinate itself. It is reserved with children and wary of strangers.
Life Expectancy: About twelve years.

Hunting and Stock Dogs

Apart from the dogs mentioned here, there are other breeds suitable for hunting, such as various hounds, terriers, and retrievers. The hunting breeds described here include only the most common.

Bernese Mountain Dog

Photo, page 37

Height/Weight: Male: 23 to 27.5 inches; to 70 pounds or more. Female: 21 to 26 inches at shoulder; to 65 pounds.
Color: Jet black with bright russet or tan markings on legs, cheeks, and above the eyes; white on the face (blaze) and chest and often some white on the feet and the tip of the tail.
Suitable: A watchdog for a house or farm, for herding cattle, and as a protecting companion on walks. If specially trained it also makes a good Seeing Eye dog or an avalanche dog.
Less Suitable: Small apartment or city life.
Needs: Freedom to romp; should be able to live in a large apartment or, better yet, in a house with a yard. It can also be kept in a large run. Even if it spends most of its time outdoors, it should be taken for at least a one-hour walk daily. Regular grooming absolutely essential (the more often it is done, the easier the chore).
Good Points: A large, easy-going dog not given to extremes of temperament. It is reliable, a willing worker, easy to lead, and faithful. With children it is kind, quiet, and long-suffering. It will announce anything that appears suspicious but does not bark a lot and is not given to biting, although it can nip swiftly if necessary.
Drawbacks: In spite of all its good qualities it can sometimes be willful and stubborn.
Life Expectancy: About twelve years.

Collie

Photo, page 37

Height/Weight: Male: 24 to 26 inches at the shoulder; 60 to 75 pounds. Female: 22 to 24 inches; 50 to 65 pounds.
Color: Solid fawn; bicolored: white and sandy yellow to mahogany red or grayish brown; tricolored: black, white, and fawn or grayish brown; also, black, white, and blue merle.
Suitable: Individuals and families with or without children who enjoy spending time with their dog.

Less Suitable: People who live in cramped quarters and devotees of dog movies who see a Lassie in every collie and expect the dog to act according to human criteria.
Needs: Lots of room in a spacious apartment and, if possible, access to a yard. Needs regular and extensive outdoor activity. Must be trained with patience and empathy. The daily grooming requires much time and patience.
Good Points: The collie has not only fine, aristocratic looks, intelligence, and a highly developed guarding instinct, but is also good with children. It is a friendly, sociable, affectionate, and attentive dog that learns easily. Does not tend to obesity.
Drawbacks: Sheds heavily. Grooming is a tedious, time-consuming chore. Collies bark a lot and loudly.
Life Expectancy: About fifteen years.
Consider Before You Buy: Overbred collies can be high-strung, timid, hysterical, obstinate, and occasionally vicious if trained by the wrong person. Ask for names of reliable breeders from the Collie Club of America, Inc. (address, page 135).

German Short-Haired Pointer

Photo, page 38

Closely related: German long-haired pointer, German wirehaired pointer, and stichelhaar.

Height/Weight: Short-haired, 24 to 25.5 inches; 55 to 70 pounds. Long-haired, 24 to 28 inches; 55 to 62 pounds. Wire-haired, 24 to 26.5 inches; 60 to 70 pounds. Stichelhaar, 25 to 26 inches; 55 to 66 pounds. Females a little less.
Color: Short-haired: solid liver to black or one of these colors with white spots or patches (black dogs may have brownish yellow markings on face and paws); also, white with liver or black spots or patches as well as black or brown ticked with white. Long-haired: solid liver, also with white or liver-and-white spot on chest; liver and white; liver ticked with white. Wire-haired: dark chestnut to medium brown; brown or black ticked with white. Stichelhaar: liver and white; liver ticked with white, with or without white patches.
Suitable: Game wardens and hunters.
Less Suitable: Life as a household pet.
Needs: Specialized training for hunting (information available from appropriate associations; addresses, page 000); as much time in the field as possible; plenty of activity and movement, especially outside the hunting season. Spacious apartment, preferably with access to a yard, but is best kept in a run.
Good Points: All types are excellent pointers; they have keen noses and perform well in all hunting tasks. They adapt well to any climate and terrain, are even-tempered, rugged, lively, docile, learn easily, and are very attached to their masters.
Drawbacks: Although good with children and a good watchdog, this breed is not really satisfied or happy when used exclusively as a family pet. If not active enough or fed a diet too high in calories, German pointers tend to get too heavy.
Life Expectancy: About twelve years.

The German spaniel's original use was to retrieve game in the ancient sport of falconry.

German Spaniel (Wachtelhund)

Drawing above

Height/Weight: All: 18 to 20.5 inches; about 40 pounds.
Color: Solid dark to reddish brown; brown with white or rust red markings on chest and toes; brown

ticked (with brown patches); pied brown and white; tricolored with brown as ground color and red and tan markings around the eyes, and on the muzzle, throat, chest, legs, and vent.
Suitable: Only for hunters. The German spaniel is an excellent all-around hunting dog that can do everything but point and is at home in any terrain. Not known in the United States.
Less Suitable: Life as a family dog without any chance to hunt.
Needs: An experienced hunter as a master and a good education in hunting. Should be kept in a run during the day and indoors at night. Needs to be groomed briefly once a day and more intensively (including checking the ears) twice a week.
Good Points: Very attached to and docile toward its master; avid and keen hunter; especially good for fox and rabbit hunting.
Drawbacks: If forced to live as a household pet with "nothing to do," it languishes; and if it does not get enough exercise it tends to get fat.
Life Expectancy: Twelve to fourteen years.

Golden Retriever

Photo, page 37

Height/Weight: Male: 23 to 24 inches; about 64 to 70 pounds. Female: 21.5 to 22.5 inches; 60–70 pounds.
Color: Gold, cream, or wheat colored (a red or mahogany tinge is undesirable according to the standard. Further white markings to be faulted).
Suitable: Flushing and retrieving game birds and water fowl, but also makes a pleasant and quiet family dog.
Less Suitable: A small apartment or a very neat household.
Needs: A large apartment and, if possible, a yard. Also, a daily walk in any weather and, if at all feasible, training and use as a hunting dog. It needs a lot of affection, and its coat should be brushed and combed carefully every day. Grooming is especially time-consuming after outings during wet weather.
Good Points: Easy to train, very affectionate, kindly, and excellent with children. The golden retriever is both a beautiful, friendly, and gentle family dog and a very lively assistant on the hunt, shunning neither work nor water. It can also be trained to become a Seeing Eye dog.
Drawbacks: Although its coat is water-repellent, it brings a lot of dirt into the house during wet weather and it sheds quite heavily.
Life Expectancy: About twelve to fifteen years.

Komondor

Photo, page 19

Hungarian herding dog

Height/Weight: Male: 25.5 to 31.5 inches. Female: 23.5 to 28 inches. All: up to about 132 pounds.
Color: White. Any color other than white is disqualifying. The skin is gray. Pink skin is less desirable, but is acceptable if there is no evidence of albinism. The nose, lips, outlines of eyelids, and pads are dark or gray. It is good if the gums and palate are also dark.
Suitable: Farms, where it herds sheep and cattle and acts as guard.
Less Suitable: Apartment and city life, an existence that people have unfortunately begun to impose on this dog.
Needs: A master who has experience with herding dogs and can offer it the opportunity to herd and protect even large herds. Best kept in a run; should not be brushed or combed but bathed once or twice a year. This type of dog should spend as much time as possible outside but does not enjoy extensive outings.
Good Points: Needs hardly any grooming but should have the ears checked and cleaned frequently. Sheds very little. Is docile and devoted to its master but savage toward large and small marauders endangering its herd. Is not intimidated even by wolves and bears but never attacks without provocation. Excellent watchdog.

Drawbacks: The long, thick fur is either shaggy or mats into cords and looks like a mop and attracts not only dirt but also parasites. The dog should therefore be checked frequently for ticks and other pests, which should be promptly removed (page 33). Far from ideal for an apartment, let alone the city.
Life Expectancy: Ten to twelve years.

The kuvasz is a reliable herding dog and a good watchdog. It needs a master with a firm hand—and plenty of space.

Kuvasz

Drawing, above

Hungarian herding dog

Height/Weight: Male: 28 to 30 inches; 100 to 115 pounds. Female: 26 to 28 inches; 70 to 90 pounds.
Color: Pure white. No markings.
Suitable: Farms or families living in the country.
Less Suitable: City life.
Needs: Like all large herding dogs, the kuvasz should have work as a herder or at least live in the country and accompany its master on walks or horseback rides. It can be kept either in a run or indoors. It has no overwhelming need for movement but should spend a good deal of its time outdoors. It is a one-master dog that needs a firm master it can respect. Its education requires someone well-versed with dogs. The more often and thoroughly its coat is brushed and curried, the less time and effort is required for this chore.
Good Points: The kuvasz is not only a dependable herding dog but also an excellent watchdog, which, given the appropriate training, will make a good guard dog. It is a large, beautiful companion with a kindly nature. Good with children, it is also courageous and not excitable. It serves its master faithfully but is suspicious of strangers. The kuvasz can stand up to any weather.
Drawbacks: Because of its size and love for freedom it is not ideal for just anybody. Also, it is not meant for living in an upstairs apartment or in the city. It is quite expensive to feed.
Life Expectancy: About twelve to fourteen years.

Münsterländer

Photo, page 37

Grosser (large) and kleiner (small) Münsterländer

Height/Weight: Large, 23 to 26 inches; about 55 pounds. Small: male, 20.5 to 22 inches; female, 17 to 20.5 inches; about 44 pounds.
Color: Grosser Münsterländer: white with black spots and patches; also black and white mixed. Kleiner Münsterländer: white with brown spots and patches; white with tan markings; and brown and white mixed.
Suitable: An all-around hunting dog. It has excellent tracking abilities and likes to retrieve. The grosser Münsterländer is also a good watchdog. It should be kept in a run. The kleiner Münsterländer makes a good household pet and companion on walks and can be kept in a spacious apartment as long as it has enough daily exercise.
Less Suitable: People who live near woods but have no interest in hunting. Such people would do better to choose a dog with as little hunting instinct as possible.
Needs: The grosser Münsterländer is happiest if it

s taken along hunting; the responsive kleiner
Münsterländer can also be managed by less experi-
nced hunters and serves well as a household pet
nd walking companion. Both strains need thorough
hough relatively simple grooming.
ood Points: Brave, intelligent, steady, docile,
nd devoted. Likes water and retrieving. Good
atchdog qualities.
rawbacks: Because of its passion for hunting it
ust be kept under restraint so that it will not roam
nd go after game. Neither breed has yet been
ccepted outside Europe.
ife Expectancy: About twelve years.

Old English Sheepdog

obtail

Photo on inside back cover

eight/Weight: All dogs, 22 to 25 inches; males
eigh to 65 pounds; females to 60 pounds.
olor: Any shade of gray, grizzle, blue or blue
erle with or without white markings or in reverse.
ny shade of brown or fawn considered distinctly
bjectionable and not encouraged.
uitable: Large families that have lots of room and
ant a large, cuddly dog.
ess Suitable: Small apartments and people with a
hobia about germs.
eeds: An apartment of reasonable size and access
 a yard, plenty of time outside, and a good walk
very day.
ood Points: Excellent herding and watchdog with
n elegant, smooth gait and a mellifluous voice,
ough it does not bark needlessly. Intelligent, easy
 teach, good-natured, and docile; especially good
ith children.
rawbacks: This large bundle of thick, long fur is
 source of dirt that considerably augments house-
ork. Grooming (thorough daily combing neces-
ary to prevent matting) is time-consuming and
rduous.
ife Expectancy: Twelve to sixteen years.

Pointer

Photo, page 37, and drawing, below

Height/Weight: Male: 25 to 28 inches; 55 to 75 pounds. Female: 23 to 26 inches; 45 to 65 pounds.
Color: Solid black, liver, orange, lemon; more commonly, spots and patches of one or two of these colors on white.
Suitable: Hunters primarily, though the pointer, being docile and friendly with children, also adjusts to life as a family dog.
Less Suitable: People not interested in hunting who want to keep it as a household pet without any chance to go hunting. Not a good city dog!
Needs: Plenty of room to move about in; should therefore preferably live in a house with a yard. Needs an experienced hunter as its master, someone who can give it proper training for hunting and takes it into the field as much as possible. The pointer needs a good run every day. Time spent on grooming is minimal.
Good Points: Noble, intelligent, and clean, the pointer is an avid hunter that locates and points game and is used primarily for hunting birds and other game.
Drawbacks: It languishes if kept merely as a family pet without outdoor activity because its hunting instinct is very pronounced.
Life Expectancy: About ten to twelve years.

It is essential that pointers receive training in hunting skills and be used for hunting all their lives.

Descriptions of Dog Breeds

Setter

Photo, page 37

English, Gordon and Irish setters

Height/Weight: English setter: 26 to 27 inches; 60 to 66 pounds. Gordon setter: 24 to 27 inches; about 55 to 80 pounds. Irish setter: 21 to 27 inches; 50 to 70 pounds. The females are often somewhat smaller (23 to 26 inches) and lighter (45 to 70 pounds).
Color: English setter: white with black, lemon, orange, or chestnut spots (and sometimes patches); also tricolored black, white, and tan. Gordon setter: Coal black with mahogany markings; sometimes with a small white mark on the chest. Irish setter: bright mahogany red.
Suitable: "Aristocratic" people, hunters, and families who love sports.
Less Suitable: High-strung or hectic people.
Needs: At least a fair-sized apartment or, preferably, a house with a garden; also, as much exercise as possible and lots of affection. Its coat should be well-combed (perhaps even curried) and brushed every day so that it will not get matted. Looking after the ears is important, too.
Good Points: It is disciplined and loyal, especially with its master. It is also sensitive and friendly, yet energetic. If it is trained, it is also a versatile helper on the hunt, working both in the field and in the water. Setters are friendly and patient with children and are generally healthy dogs.
Drawbacks: Setters like to roam, shed quite heavily, and usually do not like to ride in cars. They are also not totally reliable watchdogs. Being rather gluttonous, they also tend to get fat.
Life Expectancy: Fourteen to sixteen years; with excellent care, sometimes up to twenty years.

Working Dogs

Boxer

Photo, page 56

Height/Weight: Male: 22.5 to 25 inches; 66 to 75 pounds. Female: 21 to 23.5 inches; 60 to 70 pounds.
Color: The colors are fawn to brindle; fawn in various shades from light tan to dark deer red or mahogany, the deeper colors preferred. The brindle variety should have clearly defined black stripes on fawn background.
Suitable: Families and people who spend a lot of time with children.
Less Suitable: Sedentary people who like peace and quiet and for those with little physical strength. Not for elegant homes.
Needs: A spacious apartment; regular, not too short walks; and lots of love. Must be trained with consistency and liberal praise. Grooming is uncomplicated.
Good Points: This is a true family dog that likes to be included in everything and is very fond of children. A good watchdog, intelligent, eager to learn, courageous, very strong and spirited, but good-natured and straightforward. Can be trained for specific working skills.
Drawbacks: Boxers are subject to rheumatism and therefore should be dried off well after walks in the rain. If not trained properly, they may develop a tendency to roam and get into fights. Small children should never hold one of these "bundles of muscle" on a leash by themselves. Also, a boxer's energetic displays of affection can sometimes become a nuisance.
Life Expectancy: Often no more than eight to ten years.
Consider Before You Buy: When excited or after a workout, many boxers salivate heavily even though breeders have been trying for some time to eliminate this trait. Also, this dog usually has a short life span and tends in later years to develop tumors.

Medium-sized and small dogs.
Above left: French bulldog (bully); above right: pugs.
Center left: dark short-haired dachshund; center right: Welsh corgi, Cardigan.
Below left: basset hound; below right: beagle.

Descriptions of Dog Breeds

Doberman Pinscher

Photo, page 56

Height/Weight: Male: at the withers, 26 to 28 inches; ideal about 27.5 inches; 66 to 75 pounds. Female: 24 to 26 inches, ideal about 25.5 inches; to 58 pounds.
Color: Black, red, blue, and fawn (Isabella). Markings: rust, sharply defined, appearing above each eye and on muzzle, throat, and forechest, on all legs and feet, and below tail.
Suitable: Guards and police but also for families with at least one member who is willing and able to train the dog with absolute consistency (advance training is desirable) and keep it under discipline.
Less Suitable: People who are still neophytes in the area of dog training or who are not interested in sports or are excessively timid.
Needs: Preferably a house with a yard, but it can also be kept in a run. Requires a good education, plenty of ongoing training, and something to do, also long daily walks. Grooming is no problem.
Good Points: Dobermans become very attached to their families and generally like children, but they have little inclination for play. They prefer being given serious work to do. If trained properly, they make excellent guard and attack dogs that would not hesitate risking their lives to protect their families. Females are calmer and less aggressive than males.
Drawbacks: If a Doberman does not have an authoritative master or does not get enough exercise and work, its excess energies are almost impossible to restrain. It can then become excessively irritable, have fits of aggression, and become very dangerous because it may bite without provocation.
Life Expectancy: Twelve to fifteen years.

A wirehaired dachshund puppy being groomed. Children who grow up with a dog will always get along well with animals.

German shepherd

Photos, page 55 and back cover

Short-haired and long-haired

Height/Weight: Male: 24 to 26 inches; 65 to 85 pounds. Female: 22 to 24 inches; to 70 pounds.
Color: Solid black, gray, tan, reddish tan, reddish brown; usually with brown, tan, or whitish gray markings. Most commonly reddish brown to tan with a black back.
Suitable: Performing all kinds of services for people, such as watchdog, attack, search, rescue, or Seeing Eye dog. Ideal for policemen, guards, and people who like to spend time training their dogs and working with them.
Less Suitable: Those who enjoy a quiet life above all else or older people. This is no dog for a beginner.
Needs: A large apartment or, if possible, a house with a yard. Can also be kept in a run. Needs a very consistent master to whom it can subordinate itself. Needs plenty of work and challenge because it is eager to prove itself. German shepherds must be trained very carefully and need continued practice in skills. They also require lots of exercise. The time spent on grooming is relatively minimal. Only

German shepherds can become Seeing-Eye dogs if they are trained by specialists in this field.

the long-haired strain is regularly brushed and curried.
Good Points: This "jack-of-all-trades" is courageous, intelligent, willing, docile, and learns easily. It stands by its master loyally and reliably in any situation, accepts its place in the family readily, and likes children.
Drawbacks: If inadequately trained, this dog can become undependable and develop a tendency to pick fights with other dogs. Its tolerance for other animals and its good behavior toward people disappear, and it can become unpredictable and aggressive.
Life Expectancy: About fourteen years.
Consider Before You Buy: Beware of degenerative traits caused by wrong breeding! Such animals will attack defenseless puppies – contrary to the innate behavior of the species – and can, when fully grown, be dangerous to people. Get a list of reputable breeders from the German Shepherd Club of America (page 135).

Rottweiler

Photo, page 56

Height/Weight: Shoulder height for males, 23¾ to 27 inches; for females, 21¾ to 25¾ inches, but height should always be considered in relation to the general appearance and conformation of the dog. Males about 90 pounds; females, to 85 pounds.
Color: Coal black with clearly defined auburn markings over the eyes, on the cheeks and muzzle, chest, legs, and below the base of the tail.
Suitable: Butchers and cattle dealers (the traditional uses of this dog) but also for active families with or without children.
Less Suitable: Physically frail people and confirmed stay-at-homes.
Needs: Spacious apartment or a house with a yard, but this dog is best kept in a run. Grooming is uncomplicated and takes next to no time. This dog needs a lot of exercise and something to do. Regular walks and, if possible, regular workouts are required.
Good Points: An even-tempered, calm, obedient dog that likes children but that can, if trained for the purpose, be used as a guard or attack dog. Learns easily, is of robust constitution, does not bark without cause, roam, or go after game. Bites only if its master is in danger.
Drawbacks: This dog should be kept only by people in good physical condition and with previous experience with dogs. Children should never be allowed to take it out alone.
Life Expectancy: About ten years.
Consider Before You Buy: Watch out for dogs with serious character defects! These animals can be unpredictably aggressive and bite without provocation. Get a list of reputable breeders from the AKC (page 132).

Schnauzer

Photo, page 56; drawing, page 49
Miniature, Standard, and Giant

Height/Weight: Miniature: 12 to 14 inches; ideal size, 13.5 inches; 17 to 18 pounds. Standard: 17.5 to 18.5 inches; 33 to 40 pounds. Giant: the height of the withers of the male is 25.5 to 27.5 inches, and of the females, 23.5 to 25.5 inches, with the medians desired; about 70 to 84 pounds.
Color: Solid black, silver; also pepper-and-salt.
Suitable: People who want a dog as protection or families with children who desire an energetic rather than a fashionable dog yet one that is also docile and able to learn.
Less Suitable: Undecisive, unassertive, or very soft-hearted people.
Needs: Depending on the size of the breed, a small, fair-sized, or large apartment. A giant schnauzer can be housed in a run, but if kept indoors should be able to live in a house with a yard. All schnauzer require a good deal of exercise and things to keep them busy. The coat needs regular grooming and should be clipped and trimmed at least twice a year.

Good Points: Excellent watchdog and a courageous defender of its home and people; very affectionate disposition. Patient and friendly with children.
Drawbacks: Miniature schnauzers sometimes attack not only strangers but also familiar people when they approach members of the dog's family or the family's property.
Life Expectancy: Fourteen to sixteen years.
Consider Before You Buy: Giant schnauzers are not recommended for the novice dog owner because they need to be kept busy and should perform some obedience exercises, preferably every day. Otherwise, the buildup of aggressive energies can lead to problems.

Siberian Husky (Photos, page 56 and on back cover; drawing, below)

Height/Weight: Male: 21 to 23.5 inches at the withers; 45 to 60 pounds. Female: 20 to 22 inches at the withers; 35 to 50 pounds.
Color: Wolf gray, silver gray, tan, brown, black with white tipping, solid white; often with markings on the head, including many striking patterns not found in other breeds.
Suitable: Active people and especially those engaging in winter sports, that is, people who desire an uncomplicated, hardy, and fast dog that can take part in their winter sports activities.
Less Suitable: More sedentary types and stay-at-homes.
Needs: It does not require spacious living quarters but does need lots of freedom outside. Can be kept in a run, and even a small apartment will do. Needs a strong master whom it accepts and obeys and who will spend a lot of time with it outdoors (regardless of weather). I highly recommend that owners of Siberian huskies join an appropriate club (Addresses, page 136). The daily grooming is not time-consuming. Because of their great need for exercise, huskies use up a lot of energy, particularly in the winter, and therefore require more fats in their diet than most dogs.
Good Points: The husky has great physical endurance and is robust, affectionate, fond of children,

Siberian huskies used to be—and still are—crucial to the survival of people living in the Arctic. In more temperate climates they are popular for sled races.

and sociable. It thrives in all kinds of weather and is used in Russia and Alaska as a sled dog. Very fast and powerful for a relatively light dog. Also makes a good watchdog.
Drawbacks: Since the hierarchy of rank plays a very important role for this dog, encounters with other dogs can lead to contests of strength.
Life Expectancy: Ten to fourteen years.

Spitz Group

Photo, page 56; drawing, right

Pomeranian, keeshond, and wolfsspitz

Height/Weight: The weight of a Pomeranian for exhibition is 3 to 7 pounds. The ideal size for show specimens is from 4 to 5 pounds. Keeshond: male, 18 inches; female, 17 inches; about 50 pounds. Wolfsspitz: 18 to 22 inches; 55 to 61 pounds.
Color: Pomeranian: Acceptable colors to be judged on an equal basis; any solid color, any solid color with lighter or darker shadings of the same color, any solid color with sable or black shadings, parti-color, sable and black, and tan. Keeshond: A mixture of gray and black, solid white, and dark brown. Wolfsspitz: Silver gray, running to black in parts of the body, with a lighter shade on muzzle, stomach, legs, and tail.
Suitable: People without close neighbors who might object to the frequent barking.
Less Suitable: People with shaky nerves or those who cannot stand to have dog hair on the living-room carpet.
Needs: Space according to its size, ranging from a city apartment to a house in the country. Also needs to be kept busy and should have something it can guard and defend. Regular grooming necessary.
Good Points: Is very devoted to its family and to children; a reliable watchdog that gets attached to its home and its territory and defends them well. An intelligent, lively, and loyal dog that likes to be taught.
Drawbacks: This type of dog sheds heavily and likes to bark; the smaller it is; the more it barks.

Members of the spitz group are incorruptible watchdogs for farm, house, or apartment. They will announce anything unfamiliar promptly and loudly, whether it be a car, a bicycle, or merely a shopping bag.

Must be brushed and curried as often as possible. Pomeranians tend to suffer from intestinal problem and their diets therefore should be watched carefully.
Life Expectancy: Twelve to fourteen years, sometimes more.

Medium-Sized Dogs

Basset Hound

Photo, page 109

Height/Weight: About 12 to 15 inches; male, to 45 pounds; female, to 35 pounds.
Color: Usually white with black, sand-colored, or reddish brown patches: also tricolored: black-white-reddish brown or black-white-sand-colored. The distribution of color and markings is of no importance in judging.
Suitable: Physically healthy and psychologically stable people with a sense of humor, that is, people who are not easily upset.
Less Suitable: The average person, for frail or old people, or for anyone who does not feel drawn to a dog of real originality and with a good dose of stubbornness.

Needs: Although not large, the basset hound needs a home of generous proportions because of its long body. It also needs a daily walk of at least one hour, and its ears must be checked conscientiously. Grooming is unproblematic. Since it is somewhat awkward in its movements as it is, its weight and caloric intake should be watched.
Good Points: A good-natured, gentle, and sensitive dog but not at all timid. Devoted to its master, friendly with children, but suspicious of strangers. Mentally and physically stable and very hardy. It is by nature very reluctant to bite.
Drawbacks: Can be very obstinate. Resists teaching and tends to become overweight if it does not get enough exercise. Does not like to be alone. Not a watchdog.
Life Expectancy: Twelve to fourteen years.
Consider Before You Buy: Basset hounds tend to get kidney stones, which usually require surgery.

Chow Chow

Photo, page 73

Height/Weight: Not under 18 inches and preferably 20 to 24 inches; 40 to 50 pounds.
Color: Solid black, blue, red, cream, tan, silver, white (it may be any clear color, solid throughout, with lighter shadings on ruff, tail, and breechings). Tongue and lips must be bluish black.
Suitable: Primarily for quiet individuals who live alone, have an affinity for dogs, and choose to have a large, strong dog even if they should happen to live in a city.
Less Suitable: People who expect a dog not to have a will of its own and want a subordinate that carries out orders on command. Not a dog for a beginner.
Needs: An apartment of at least moderate size but can also be kept in a run, especially because it is often uncomfortable in centrally heated rooms. Requires an understanding but consistent person and thorough daily grooming. Does not have a great desire for movement but should be taken for walks more frequently in the summer.
Good Points: Accepts only one master whom it obeys – though sometimes rather reluctantly – and is very loyal to. An intelligent and dignified dog with a face that is not easy to read; a watchdog, but not loud.
Drawbacks: A one-person dog, the chow responds to the rest of the family with friendly reserve or indifference and is unfriendly towards strangers. It does not think much of games or of children, and it hates muzzles and leashes. A harness is advisable.
Life Expectancy: Fourteen to sixteen years.

Cocker Spaniel

American and English

Photo, pages 73, 74, 99; drawing, below

Height/Weight: American: male, not over 15.5 inches; female, not over 14.5 inches. English: male, 16 to 17 inches; female, 15 to 16 inches. Males, 28 to 34 pounds; females: 26 to 32 pounds.
Color: Solid black, red (or golden), and brown; the American cocker spaniel can have some white on the neck and chest. Bicolored: black and tan, black and white, brown and white, orange and white, and liver and brown; orange, brown, blue-black flecked with white. Tricolored: black and white with tan as well as all the flecked colors with tan. The American spaniel occurs in all these colors and in silver buff.

If you have a cocker spaniel, get it a tall food dish that narrows toward the top. This way it will keep from dunking its ears in the food.

Suitable: Sensitive people who, however, know how to assert themselves.
Less Suitable: People who confuse authority with harshness, fanatics about cleanliness, and those who think thorough grooming is unnecessary and therefore leave the care of the coat up to the animal.
Needs: Moderately large home, preferably with the use of a yard, and a daily walk. Quite a bit of time for training and grooming (should be regularly curried, thoroughly combed, and brushed). Because cocker spaniels tend to get eczema on their flews, food remains should be carefully removed from the mouth area with a cloth after every meal. Their long lop ears should be checked and cleaned frequently.
Good Points: Very affectionate and sensitive but physically robust and fond of water. When kept indoors, the cocker displays restraint and barks little. Gets along well with children.
Drawbacks: Not a reliable watchdog. When its hunting instincts are awakened, as by the scent of a wild animal, all its obedience training is forgotten. It enjoys food, tends to get overweight, and then gets lazy and prone to illness. Give it plenty of low-calorie food, and check its weight frequently.
Life Expectancy: Fourteen to sixteen years.
Consider Before You Buy: Among solid red and black cocker spaniels there are occasionally over-bred individuals with behavioral problems. Such dogs tend to bite, sometimes even their masters. Get a list of reputable breeders from the American Spaniel Club before you buy your dog (Addresses, page 132).

Dalmatian

Photo, page 73

Height/Weight: The desirable height is between 19 and 23 inches at the withers, and any dog over 24 inches at the withers is disqualified. Weight: about 55 pounds.
Color: Black and/or liver patches and dots on pure white; the denser the spots, the better.
Suitable: Families, especially with children, that enjoy such sports as hiking, jogging, bicycling, and horseback riding.
Less Suitable: Stay-at-homes and people with psychologic problems.
Needs: An apartment that is not too small, preferably with access to a yard. Relatively little care but lots of exercise. Also needs a lot of affection because it tends to get melancholy otherwise.
Good Points: Easily trained, loyal, and always in a good mood. Likes to play with children. Very clean and alert and without a great passion for hunting.
Drawbacks: Easily upset by disagreements in "its" family. If treated unjustly, it will bear a grudge for years.
Life Expectancy: About twelve years.
Consider Before You Buy: Blue-eyed puppies and their littermates often have hearing defects or are deaf.

English Bulldog

Drawing, page 117

Height/Weight: Height, 16 to 18 inches. The weight for mature males is about 50 pounds; for mature females, about 40 pounds.
Color: Solid white, red, reddish to pale tan; these colors piebald, streaked, or sprinkled with white. Often with a black mask or a black muzzle.
Suitable: People who like something different and prefer this rather sullen-looking stocky fellow to the kind of dog most people consider more attractive.
Less Suitable: Keeping in a walk-up apartment.
Needs: Loving people, a daily, though not very long walk. Grooming is unproblematic. Its food (mostly meat) should not be too high in calories because this dog, which is not fond of exertion, tends to get fat. It can be kept in a small apartment. If raised with love and patience, it develops into a very docile and affectionate dog.
Good Points: Dignified and restrained, good-natured, and reliable. A faithful and clean dog,

The English bulldog used to be trained for dogfighting, which is probably why it was depicted in the masthead of the German satirical weekly on political affairs, *Simplicissimus*. Today the English bulldog is a good-natured family dog.

fond of its home, and, considering its bulk, sometimes surprisingly active and agile. Also very fond of children. Shows more interest in "its" humans than in other dogs.
Drawbacks: Breathes loudly, snores, and is uncomfortable in the heat. If given too much food and not enough exercise, it tends to get fat. Because of the broad head of the breed, the puppies must often be delivered by cesarean section.
Life Expectancy: Nine to twelve years.

Kromfohrländer

Photo, page 73

Height/Weight: From 15 to 18 inches; 26 to 31 pounds.
Color: Pure white with areas of different shades of brown around eyes and ears, the top of the head, and the back, the saddle marked off by white stripes.
Suitable: Families with children wanting a sympathetic, medium-sized dog that not everybody else has.
Less Suitable: Anybody interested only in well-established breeds.
Needs: It will make do with even a small apartment. Must be combed and brushed daily, but this is not very time-consuming.
Good Points: This is a very pleasant and intelligent family dog that likes children. It is spirited but never jumpy. A very good watchdog, faithful, obedient, and easy to train. This breed is fast gaining in popularity in Germany, and since its acceptance by the Fédération Cynologique Internationale (FCI), is becoming known in other European countries.
Drawbacks: Like the fox terrier, which is one of its ancestors, the Kromfohrländer sometimes exhibits a tendency to initiate fights with other dogs.
Life Expectancy: Sixteen to eighteen years.

Poodle

Photo, page 73; drawing, below

Toy, Miniature, and Standard

Height/Weight: Toy: 10 inches or under at the highest point of the shoulders; 15 pounds. Miniature: 15 inches or under at the highest point of the shoulders; 25 pounds. Standard: over 15 inches; any poodle that is 15 inches or less is disqualified from competition as a standard poodle; 45 pounds.
Color: The coat is an even and solid color at the skin. In blues, grays, silvers, browns, café-au-laits, apricots, and creams, the coat may show varying shades of the same color. This is frequently present in the somewhat darker feathering of the

The poodle (here in the puppy clip) is a family dog, affectionate, friendly, frisky, and very easy to teach.

ears and in the tipping of the ruff. Particolored dogs (not an even solid color at the skin but of two or more colors) are disqualified.
Suitable: Both people living alone and families with children, that is, anyone who wants a beautiful and intelligent dog that is a whiz at learning.
Less Suitable: People who try to exploit the poodle's justly famous talent for learning and consequently ask too much of the dog, and the impatient, who think training a dogs means whipping it into shape.
Needs: Enough space for its size in a small, average, or large home. Daily walks, play, and other time spent with people. Thorough combing and brushing, preferably every day. Should be professionally bathed and clipped at least every six to eight weeks.
Good Points: It has classic good looks and is affectionate and outgoing. It quickly grasps what it is supposed to learn, likes to play with children, and hardly sheds.
Drawbacks: Grooming a poodle requires a lot of time and patience and/or a good poodle parlor. (You have to figure on about three hours for bathing, drying, brushing, combing, clipping, and shaping.)
Life Expectancy: About twelve years.
Consider Before You Buy: Very small toys often show physical and psychologic signs of degeneration and may develop into neurotic, hysterical yappers and nippers.

Whippet

Drawing, right

Height/Weight: Male: 18 to 22 inches; to 28 pounds. Female: 18 to 21 inches; to 20 pounds.
Color: Immaterial, but often from black to gray; also, reddish gray and beige; also, a mixture of these colors. Often with white markings on the head, chest, and feet.
Suitable: Active people with a flair for elegance.
Less Suitable: Those attached to the comforts of home and people who see the graceful whippet primarily as an elegant piece of decor.
Needs: A great deal of exercise; should be able to run free and fast as much as feasible. When racing (for information, inquire at an appropriate dog club, address on page 134), the whippet can reach speeds up to 37.5 miles per hour (60 kilometers per hour). The only grooming required is brushing and an occasional rubbing down with a dampened piece of soft leather.
Good Points: The whippet is a cheerful and affectionate house dog and companion for outings (it also likes to run along beside a bicycle). It has almost aristocratic looks but a simple-hearted nature. It is intelligent, docile, and very clean. If given daily exercise it can be kept in a relatively small apartment, though preferably with access to the outside. If it has had a good run to work off its excess energies, it will then be quiet and contented at home. It does not bark much but does respond to suspicious-sounding noises. Its short, fine fur requires little care. In spite of its delicate looks, this is a robust dog that seldom gets sick.
Drawbacks: Although generally hardy, the whippet is sensitive to the cold and the damp. It should therefore wear a sweater in the winter and a raincoat in bad weather.
Life Expectancy: If properly kept, often over fifteen years.

Like all greyhounds, the whippet carries its tail between its legs except for running, when the tail is extended horizontally.

Terriers

Airedale Terrier

Photo, page 100

Height/Weight: From 22 to 23 inches; male, to 50 pounds; female, to 45 pounds.
Color: Black and tan, or tan and dark grizzle.
Suitable: Fanciers of large dogs wanting a good-natured dog that likes children and likes to protect the family.
Less Suitable: Small apartments and older people.
Needs: An apartment of at least moderate size, preferably with access to a yard. Regular, long walks. Must be kept busy. Likes to play and swim. Should be trimmed every four months.
Good Points: Lively but patient family dog. Affectionate, learns well, and a watchdog but not loud. If treated with love, totally cooperative. Can be used as a guard dog if trained for that purpose.
Drawbacks: If kept in the house with other dogs, problems can arise because it does not like to play second fiddle.
Life Expectancy: Ten to fourteen years.

Bedlington Terrier

Drawing, right

Height/Weight: Male: 16.5 inches; 17 to 23 pounds. Female: 15.5 inches at the withers; to 22 pounds.
Color: Sandy, liver, blue, blue and tan, sandy and tan, liver and tan.
Suitable: Family dog for people who like the idea of a "lamb with the courage of a lion."
Less Suitable: Inconsistent trainers, soft-hearted people, and anyone who likes to "sic" the dog.
Needs: This dog feels happy in an apartment of moderate size. It needs a loving but consistent education and must be shorn from time to time (depending on how fast the hair grows). Lots of walking, playing, and other exercise are essential.
Good Points: Affectionate, loyal, and a good watchdog. Likes to play with children, whom it will protect and if necessary defend. Hardly sheds.
Drawbacks: This dog may look like a lamb but it is very plucky if challenged, and if incorrectly raised can become short-tempered and aggressive. Always keep it on a leash when walking with it in woods or fields because its hunting instinct is readily aroused.
Life Expectancy: Twelve to fourteen years.

This is what a Bedlington terrier looked like over a hundred years ago when people in England and Scotland used it for poaching.

Since those times, the Bedlington has been crossed with other breeds, including greyhounds (apparent in the posture of the tail), and a new clip has been invented for him that makes him look like a "lamb."

Descriptions of Dog Breeds

Boston Terrier

Height/Weight: From 12 to 17 inches; 15 to 25 pounds, but not exceeding 25 pounds, divided by classes as follows: lightweight, under 15 pounds; middleweight, 15 and under 20 pounds; heavyweight, 20 and not exceeding 25 pounds.
Color: Brindled or glossy black, with white markings on the head (often with a blaze), the throat, chest, front legs, and back legs below the hocks.
Suitable: For people living alone and families, even in the city.
Less Suitable: People with little patience, because the Boston terrier's education requires consistency and perseverance.
Needs: Daily walks, but it is not fond of long hikes. Grooming is simple: regular brushing and an occasional rubbing down with a dampened chamois cloth suffice. It needs a lot of affection and attention and is happy in a fairly small apartment.
Good Points: An intelligent and lovable companion at home and on walks, as well as a guard. It is because of these qualities that it is sometimes called "America's national dog." In the United States, its ears are clipped.
Drawbacks: Although breeders have succeeded over the last thirty years in toning down this dog's scrappy temperament (a manifestation of the bulldog and bullterrier blood in its veins), there are some individuals that like to fight and bite. Before you buy your dog, get the advice of the Boston Terrier Club of America, Inc. (address, page 138).
Life Expectancy: Ten to twelve years.

Bullterrier

Photo, page 100

Height/Weight: Male, to 22 inches; female, to 21 inches. Male, to 60 pounds; female, to 50 pounds.
Color: Solid white, black, reddish tan, brown; bicolored: black and white or brindled brownish yellow, often with white markings.
Suitable: Only experts on dogs who know how to treat them.
Less Suitable: The average man on the street and those for whom beauty is all.
Needs: Not too much space; is best kept in an apartment of average size and with access to a fenced-in yard. It needs a lot of love, which it reciprocates. Grooming is unproblematic.
Good Points: A reliable watchdog and defender that does not bark much. It has to feel its master's superiority and then is totally devoted. It is not a brawler but responds quickly and viciously if it is attacked or its master is threatened.
Drawbacks: If purchased by someone unaccustomed to dogs and if raised improperly, the bullterrier may turn into a dangerous defense agent that may decide to go into action at any time. This dog is also sensitive to the cold and to wet.
Life Expectancy: Twelve to fifteen years.

Fox Terrier

Photo, page 100; drawing, page 7

Smooth and wirehaired: Although these two strains differ only in the consistency and color of the coat, they are considered two separate breeds.

Height/Weight: Not over 15.5 inches at the withers; the female proportionately shorter; about 18 pounds in show condition; the female some 2 pounds less.
Color: Smooth: white with black and/or brown markings on head and body. Wirehaired: white with reddish brown to reddish black markings.
Suitable: Active, easy-going people – also children – who are not easily upset.
Less Suitable: Very nervous people or those who need quiet and rest.
Needs: Considering how small it is, it needs a lot of room and should be kept in a home of at least moderate size. Access to a yard is helpful. It needs lots of movement and at least one long daily walk that should include some play. The wirehaired type should be regularly trimmed with a plucking knife

and the tail clipped now and then. In the smooth type, individual hairs that grow too long are plucked with thumb and index finger. Both types should be combed and brushed daily. Their education demands utter consistency.
Good Points: High-spirited, playful, silly, easy to teach, and very fond of children. It is also robust, plucky, and an excellent guard. Its curiosity leads it to take part in anything that goes on around it.
Drawbacks: Never refuses an invitation to fight, gets jealous easily, and can be very noisy.
Life Expectancy: Twelve to fourteen years.
Consider Before You Buy: Watch out for individuals with disturbed behavior, such as excessive irritability or nervousness and aggressiveness. Ask for names of reputable breeders at the American Fox Terrier Club (page 136).

Scottish Terrier

Photo, page 100

Also known as "Scottie"

Height/Weight: From 10 to 11 inches. Male, 19 to 22 pounds; female, 18 to 21 pounds.
Color: Steel or iron gray, brindled or grizzled, black, wheaten, or sandy. White markings are not desired.
Suitable: People who want a small but very strong dog.
Less Suitable: The tender-hearted as well as proponents of antiauthoritarian education.
Needs: It will be content in a small apartment but needs a regular schedule of frequent, long walks. Because of its high-strung nature it needs gentle but energetic training. Must be brushed and combed daily and trimmed at least three times a year.
Good Points: Affectionate, funny, and cute, but totally fearless. It is playful and gets along well with children if it has been brought up with them. Good watchdog without barking a lot.
Drawbacks: Because its sympathies extend only to those close to it, it meets strangers, including children, with suspicion and often aggression. Caution is also in order when it meets other dogs, because it is not the least impressed even by dogs much larger than itself.
Life Expectancy: Ten to fourteen years.

Skye Terrier

Photo, page 100

Height/Weight: From 8.5 to 10 inches; about 25 pounds. (At the ideal height of 10 inches, the body length is over 3 feet.)
Color: All shades of gray ranging from silver to black; champagne; ideally with black points and a black mask; the ears are always black.
Suitable: Families and people living alone, including older people, who are willing to put up with some extra cleaning for the sake of this lovely and extremely pleasant companion.
Less Suitable: Pedants and those who lack patience, that is, people who should choose a dog that requires less coat care. Also not for people who live several flights up in a building without an elevator.
Needs: Though it does not require a lot of room, it can be underfoot too much in small apartments because of its excessive body length (it is almost four times as long as it is tall). It is content with a normal schedule of walks and is no friend of long hikes. The necessary daily care of the coat (currying, combing, and brushing) is both time-consuming and painstaking.
Good Points: A friendly and lively dog with good watchdog qualities. Beautiful, devoted, and patient with children, especially if it is raised with them.
Drawbacks: Its long hair drags along the ground, and it carries a lot of dirt into the house, especially in rainy weather. The whiskers and the hair around the muzzle should be cleaned after every meal. The hair below the tail also should be checked and cleaned every day. Tends to bark a lot.
Life Expectancy: Ten to fourteen years.

West Highland White Terrier

Height/Weight: About 10 to 11 inches; 17 to 19 pounds.
Color: Pure white only, with a jet-black nose.
Suitable: Cheerful individuals and familes with children who want a small, cute, and playful dog.
Less Suitable: Those who are reluctant to spend the necessary time for daily, intensive grooming.
Needs: Daily currying, combing, and brushing; regular walks (though no forced marches), playing, and lots of attention from its family. It is content in a small apartment, especially if it has access to a yard. Because it can be quite obstinate, raising it is not altogether unproblematic and requires both love and firmness.
Good Points: A robust and cute little dog with a lovely coat, easy to keep except for the time required for grooming and occasional resistance to training. It likes to play with children, is eager to learn, and develops into a pleasant and content house companion.
Drawbacks: If left alone too much, it can turn into a yapper and thus become a nuisance for the neighbors. If this tendency is discouraged from the very beginning, however, a firm word will suffice to silence it.
Life Expectancy: Twelve to fourteen years.

Yorkshire Terrier

Photo, page 100

Height/Weight: To 9 inches; male, not over 7 pounds; female, not over 6 pounds.
Color: Steel blue and tan; that is, a steel-blue cover over the back, and tan head, chest, and legs; the fur should be of a silky texture. Puppies are born black and tan.
Suitable: Terrier lovers who want a small dog and do not mind spending the time and care necessary for grooming this miniterrier.
Less Suitable: "Macho" types and children unless the dog grows up with them.
Needs: Very little space; is happy even in a small apartment. Should be thoroughly combed and brushed every day and kept very clean. To keep it from dropping over the eyes and being dipped into the food dish at mealtimes, the long hair on the head must be pinned or tied together. The Yorkshire terrier needs to be raised with love but also firmness. It likes to be outdoors but does not require long walks.
Good Points: The Yorkshire terrier is a small, lovable dog of real beauty. It is an affectionate, lively pet with modest demands, adjusting well to apartment life. It is a watchdog and mistrustful of strangers.
Drawbacks: Not overly fond of children, especially if it does not know them. Does not get along too well with other animals, either. In spite of its long hair, it is sensitive to the cold and should wear a sweater in the winter.
Life Expectancy: Twelve years.
Consider Before You Buy: The Yorkshire terrier is difficult to breed, and sometimes puny or neurotic puppies are offered for sale. Buy only from a reputable breeder! Ask the Yorkshire Terrier Club of America, Inc. to recommend breeders to you (Address, page 138).

Small Dogs

Beagle

Photo, page 109

Smaller type: Elisabeth beagle

Height/Weight: Dogs to 13 and to 15 inches; under 13 inches, to 18 pounds; over 13 inches, to 20 pounds. Elisabeth beagle: not over 12 inches; under 20 pounds.
Color: Solid black, white, tan, orange, or a combi-

nation of any two of these colors; also, tricolored black, white, and auburn; black, white, and orange; and black, white, and sandy.
Suitable: Cheerful people with or without children even if they live in a small apartment.
Less Suitable: People who want a dog as protection against burglars or people who do not want to share their dog with anybody.
Needs: Long daily walks, because it is descended from scent hounds. It feels at home anywhere, in a large or small apartment, and enjoys living with several other dogs because the natural urge to live in a pack is still strong in this breed.
Good Points: The beagle is sociable, likes children, is affectionate, easy-going, and clean, and has a pleasant voice that it does not overuse.
Drawbacks: Does not make a very good watchdog. If it is not walked enough it may develop an urge to roam. Does not form an exclusive relationship with one person but responds to anyone who pays attention to it or feeds it.
Life Expectancy: About twelve years.

Dachshund

Photos, pages 10, 38, 109, 110, and front cover; drawing, right

The Dachshund (the name means "badger dog" in German) comes with short hair, long hair, or wirehair and in *three sizes:* normal, miniature, and toy ("rabbit").

Height: Standard: about 8 to 11 inches. The standard measurement for dachshunds is, however, not height at the withers but the circumference of the chest.
Circumference of Chest/Weight: Standard: over 14 inches; 11 to 20 pounds. Miniature: 12 to 14 inches; 9 pounds. Toy ("rabbit"): under 12 inches; under 8 pounds.
Color: Black, red of various shades, brown, and these colors brindled; bicolored: black or brown with red markings, red with yellow markings; also, a bicolored mixture of the solid ground colors,

The little dachshund with its short legs and long body is a likely candidate for back problems. The skeleton that is sketched into the drawing shows what strains lever action and the force of gravity impose on this kind of body.

sometimes with white and spots of two or more colors. Wirehaired dachshunds should have no white markings.
Suitable: People who do not regard a strong will as a vice but rather as a sign of personality and would rather have an individualistic companion than a devoted slave.
Less Suitable: Someone inconsistent. The raising of a dachshund requires firmness.
Needs: Exercise and things to keep it busy to sublimate its hunting instincts. The short-haired type needs little grooming, the wirehaired type should be clipped twice a year, and the long-haired needs to be combed regularly and thoroughly and brushed.
Good Points: A sympathetic, intelligent, and uncomplicated pet for home and outings. If trained well, it learns to obey commands. Gets along well with children.
Drawbacks: Likes to dig holes in the ground outside and also scratches the floor inside. If it does not get enough exercise, it tends to get fat; susceptible to spinal problems and paralysis. Should therefore not be kept in a walk-up apartment.
Life Expectancy: Twelve to fourteen years.
Consider Before You Buy: Dachshunds sold by breeders who mass-produce them can develop into bowlegged, timid creatures. Consult the Dachshund Club of America, Inc., for a list of reputable breeders (address, page 133).

French Bulldog

Photo, page 109

Height/Weight: From 10 to 12 inches; under 22 pounds, lightweight class; 22 pounds and not over 28 pounds, heavyweight class.
Color: Pure white, grayish brown to black with white, various mixtures of black and auburn brindled, with or without white patches.
Suitable: People who would like a Great Dane but do not have the facilities to keep a large dog.
Less Suitable: People living in the top-floor apartment of a building without an elevator.
Needs: Not much room; is quite content in a small apartment, but it does need regular exercise.
Good Points: Courageous; needs love; does not require much coat care. A trustworthy companion (also for older people), a vigilant watchdog, and a passionate hunter of rats.
Drawbacks: Sensitive to the heat, snores, and wheezes. If it gets overweight, it has difficulty breathing.
Life Expectancy: Eight to ten years.

Pug

Photo, page 109

Height/Weight: Up to 11 inches; 14 to 18 pounds.
Color: Silver, apricot-fawn, beige, black face, and often a dark stripe down the back; pure black.
Suitable: People who live quiet lives (including older people) and who want an uncomplicated dog.
Less Suitable: People who want a sports-loving dog.
Needs: A little space in a small apartment will do, but it wants much love and attention. Grooming is simple, but it does need to be brushed daily.
Good Points: The pug is calm and cheerful and feels very close to its master. It likes to play, also with children, and does not bark much.
Drawbacks: If it is not given enough to do, it may become phlegmatic, but it should not be overexerted. Tends to gain too much weight if overfed. Its breathing is loud, and it snores when sleeping.
Life Expectancy: Twelve to fifteen years.

Welsh Corgi

Photo, page 109

Small Welsh shepherd. Cardigan (medium-long tail) and Pembroke (short tail)

Height/Weight: Cardigan: about 12 inches; Pembroke: 11 to 12 inches. Cardigan male, 22 to 25 pounds; female, to 20 pounds. Pembroke male, to 30 pounds; female, to 28 pounds.
Color: Cardigan: red pied with white, bluish black pied with red and white, and blue merle. Pembroke: solid red, brown to brownish gray, and black with white or red markings on head, chest, neck, and paws. Also, all the colors of the Cardigan.
Suitable: Anyone who falls in love with this small shepherd with its foxy face. Love is justified not only because it is cute to look at but also because it has an excellent character.
Less Suitable: Upstairs apartments in buildings without an elevator. Climbing stairs is harmful for this dog, with its short legs and long body.
Needs: Some task that serves as a substitute for its original duties as a herding dog, that is, something it can watch over and guard. Grooming requires little effort. Brush regularly and rub down with a slightly moistened chamois cloth to restore the natural gloss of the coat. If provided with regular exercise, this dog can be kept in a small, but not too tiny, city apartment.
Good Points: Among these are the simplicity of care required, the modest demands for housing, the dog's intelligence and eagerness to learn, and above all its charming and affectionate manner. In addition, it is not only a good watchdog but also an ideal companion for children.
Drawbacks: None, except that climbing stairs is unhealthy for it.
Life Expectancy: About fourteen years.

Descriptions of Dog Breeds

Miniatures

Chihuahua
Photo, page 127; drawing, below

Smooth coat and long coat

Height/Weight: Not over 5 inches; male, to 6 pounds; female, to 6 pounds (2 to 4 pounds preferred).
Color: Solid white, chestnut, fawn, sandy, steel blue to black; two or more of these colors piebald or with markings or splashed.
Suitable: A "lady's dog" as long as it is not overly pampered and spoiled, but also a good pet for anyone who likes diminutive things as well as for older people.
Less Suitable: People who treat it like a doll, forcing it to spend most of the time being bored in an apartment. Under these conditions, it will pine away.
Needs: It is modest in all its demands – space, care, and food. Even a small apartment will do for a home. Because of its tiny size, its coat care takes hardly any time; only the long-haired type has to be combed and brushed frequently. It does have to be walked regularly and likes to be entertained and played with at home.

The chihuahua is the smallest dog in the world, but it is more robust than it looks. It needs regular walks and wants to be kept busy.

Good Points: This is the tiniest breed now in existence, but in spite of being such a featherweight it is more robust than anyone would think, would like nothing better than to go hunting, and defends itself against bigger dogs. It is a winning, loyal, and modest pet.
Drawbacks: Tends to have teary eyes and conjunctivitis. The eyes should therefore be checked and cared for daily. It can also develop into a yapper.
Life Expectancy: Up to fourteen years and even more.

English Toy Spaniels
Drawing, below

Group: King Charles spaniels and the three variants: Prince Charles, Ruby, and Blenheim spaniels. The Cavalier King Charles spaniel also forms part of this group.

The Cavalier King Charles spaniel belongs to the group of English toy spaniels. In England it is still used for hunting.

Height/Weight: King Charles and the three variants: 10 to 13 inches; 9 to 12 pounds. Cavalier King Charles: 10 to 13.5 inches; 12 to 18 pounds.
Color: King Charles: glossy black with tan markings. Prince Charles: pearly white with coal black and red chestnut patches, head with a white blaze. Ruby: solid chestnut red without any markings. Blenheim: pearly white with yellowish red or chestnut brown patches; head with a white blaze

and a red spot centered on the top of the head. Cavalier King Charles: black and tan, tricolor (black, white, and reddish brown); also, the colors of the Blenheim and the ruby.
Suitable: Anyone who is looking for a small, sympathetic companion at home and outdoors, a dog that is not only cute to look at but is also remarkably intelligent. The Cavalier can be used for hunting on flat terrain.
Less Suitable: People who will let it spend most of its time lolling on sofas like a spoiled lap dog.
Needs: Can be kept in a small apartment; needs regular walks and a lot of affection. The care of the coat, which must be attended to regularly and thoroughly, requires a lot of time and effort. Daily combing and brushing keep the chore from becoming too arduous.
Good Points: This is a cheerful and lively dog, intelligent and easy to train. It has a gentle and agreeable character. Sometimes it acts shy with strangers. It is well-disposed toward children, especially if they belong to its family.
Drawbacks: Not a very good watchdog because it rarely barks. If it is left alone too much, it pines away. Since it is sensitive to the cold and wet, it should wear a sweater in the winter and a raincoat in bad weather. Always dry its coat thoroughly (perhaps with a hair dryer). Bathe as little as possible, but give it frequent good brushings.
Life Expectancy: Twelve to fourteen years.
Consider Before You Buy: Puppies that are born in the winter must be protected from drafts until late spring and should be kept warm.

Lhasa Apso

Photo, page 127

Small Tibetan terrier

Height/Weight: Male, 9 to 11 inches at shoulder, 11 to 15 pounds; female, slightly smaller, somewhat less heavy.
Color: Slate, honey, sandy, rust, smoke, and white; also combinations of these colors.
Suitable: Lovers of small, fuzzy dogs; also older people.
Less Suitable: People who are fussy about housekeeping.
Needs: Not much space; it feels quite comfortable in a small apartment. Needs regular though not excessively long walks and much love. Should be combed carefully every day and perhaps curried and brushed.
Good Points: A self-assured, lovable, and cheerful companion. Its great devotion is usually concentrated on one person, and it usually responds to strangers with distrust. Easy to train. Good watchdog. Can get very old.
Drawbacks: Does not always get along with children. With its long, manelike hair it brings a fair amount of dirt into the house, especially in wet weather.
Life Expectancy: Fourteen and sometimes more than sixteen years.

Maltese

Photo, page 127

Height/Weight: Male: 8.5 to 10 inches; female: 8 to 9 inches. Weight under 7 pounds with from 4 to 6 pounds preferred. Overall quality is favored over size.
Color: Pure white (light tan or lemon on the ears is permitted by judges at shows but not desirable).
Suitable: People more interested in having an exceptionally beautiful small dog rather than a practical one.
Less Suitable: Households where tidiness is of utmost importance and people who do not have time for the necessary daily grooming.

Miniatures.
Above left: long-haired chihuahua; above right: Chinese crested dog.
Center left: Maltese; center right: white Pekingese.
Below left: Lhasa Apso; below right: miniature pinscher.

Needs: Not much space but a lot of looking after. A thorough daily combing and brushing of the hair is a must. The Maltese has no great need for exercise.
Good Points: It has a dignified, "aristocratic" manner, is intelligent (and sometimes sly) and very attached to its master. Calls attention to any suspicious sound.
Drawbacks: This dog does not shed, but with its long hair that reaches down to the ground it carries a lot of dirt in, especially in wet weather. Since it is sensitive to dampness it must be rubbed and blown dry after every outing in wet weather.
Life Expectancy: Fourteen to sixteen years; sometimes lives to over eighteen years.

Mexican Hairless

Photo, page 127

Xoloitzcuintle, also Chinese crested dog and hairless dog (cane nudo; "African")

Height/Weight: From 10 to 16 inches; 18 pounds.
Color: Cane nudo: elephant gray, gray with pink patches, flesh colored with gray to black patches. Mexican hairless: reddish gray. Chinese crested: solid white to gray, black, pink, mahogany, copper, and even blue and lilac or multicolored with spots in a number of these colors.
Suitable: People who have a yen for the exotic and value the unusual over the tried and proven.
Less Suitable: People who are fond of the cold, such as practitioners of winter sports or the energy conscious, who like to turn the thermostat down.
Needs: A warm spot in a small apartment will keep it happy. It needs lots of physical as well as emotional warmth. It should wear a sweater in the winter. Its "coat" requires little care, and its need for exercise is moderate.

Apricot-colored poodle puppy. At this age it should not be clipped but should be brushed and combed thoroughly every day.

Good Points: Spirited, very devoted, cheerful, and affectionate toward members of the family, but reserved toward strangers. Good watchdog, but sometimes barks too much.
Drawbacks: Trembles a lot, partly out of nervousness and partly to keep warm. It not always fond of children.
Life Expectancy: Ten to twelve years.

Papillon

Photo, back cover

Height/Weight: Not over 11 inches. Male, 8 to 10 pounds; females, no more than 8 pounds.
Color: Solid black, brown, lemon yellow to red; also white patches with one or two of these colors.
Suitable: People who want a small dog that does not yap. Also older people.
Less Suitable: Someone looking for a watchdog that reports every sound.
Needs: Not much space; can be kept in a small apartment. Short walks satisfy it; it is no friend of long hikes. For a small dog it requires quite a lot of grooming because its long fur and the silky hair on its butterfly-wing ears must be thoroughly combed and brushed every day.
Good Points: This is a charming, lively, and even-tempered little dog, obedient, quiet, robust, and adaptable. It does not mind traveling and thrives in any climate but appreciates the atmosphere of a steady home.
Drawbacks: Not a reliable watchdog. Brings some dirt into the house, especially in bad weather.
Life Expectancy: Ten to fourteen years.

Pekingese

Photo, page 127

Height/Weight: From 8 to 9 inches; 10 to 14 pounds.
Color: All shades, ranging from white to gray and black and from beige to red; either unicolored or pied and striped; often with white markings.
Suitable: Quiet or older people who are looking for

an attractive small dog that appreciates the comforts of home and protects house and grounds.
Less Suitable: Families with several children, sports lovers, and those with little appreciation for home life.
Needs: It is satisfied to rule over a small apartment, but as a former palace dog it is also at its ease in large rooms. Regular coat care – frequent brushing and combing – is important, and it needs a lot of love and affection but should not be coddled too much.
Good Points: Fearless, conscious of its beauty, and needing to be loved, the Pekingese is usually a one-person dog. It is devoted to its master, whom it does not want to share with anybody.
Drawbacks: Its devotion and constant readiness to defend its master and the master's property can take on the form of jealousy and tyranny. Its abundant fur drags along the ground and brings a fair amount of dirt into the house.
Life Expectancy: If well cared for, fourteen to sixteen years.

Pinscher

Also: miniature pinscher

Photo, page 127
drawing, below

The Affenpinscher, not to be confused with the miniature pinscher, is a small, wirehaired dog that is very plucky. It can be kept even in a tiny apartment.

Height/Weight: Standard size: 16 to 19 inches; 26 to 35 pounds. Miniature: male, to 11.5 inches; female, to 10.5 inches. Male, to 10 pounds; female to 9 pounds.
Color: Black wth brown markings, solid fawn to red, and pepper-and-salt.
Suitable: Just about anybody and any kind of living quarters. Very popular in Europe.
Less Suitable: People with noise-sensitive neighbors.
Needs: Even a small apartment will satisfy its needs for space. It is relatively easy to train, and its coat does not need much grooming.
Good Points: An intelligent, affectionate, and very clean dog. Also a good watchdog that can defend itself with its sharp teeth if the need arises. The miniature pinscher especially can be kept in the city.
Drawbacks: Unfortunately, quite a few of these dogs are given to shrill yapping.
Life Expectancy: About fourteen to fifteen years.

Shih Tzu

Tibetan lion dog

Height/Weight: From 9 to 10.5 inches; should be no more than 11 inches nor less than 8 inches; weight of mature dogs, 12 to 15 pounds; should be no more than 18 pounds nor less than 9 pounds.
Color: Black, white, and all shades of gray, beige, red, and brown; usually two or more colors; if the ground color is dark, there is often a white blaze and the tip of the tail is white.
Suitable: People (whether alone or with a family) who have a yen for the exotic and who do not mind the prospect of years of painstaking coat care.
Less Suitable: Fanatics about cleanliness and people with neighbors who object to barking dogs.
Needs: A loving master whom it will follow devotedly. This dog's abundant coat, which reaches down to the ground, requires daily care – currying, combing, and brushing – that demands much time

.nd patience. It makes sense to confine the "lion's
nane" to the top of the head by means of hair clips
r a ribbon, especially when the dog eats. This dog
eeds daily, though not very long, walks, and
hould be kept busy and provided with play at
ome. It feels happy even in a small apartment.
;ood Points: Its small size, decorative looks, and
he legendary fame of its ancestors, which, together
vith the Pekingese, were among the favorite dogs
t the Emperor of China's court, have all contrib-
ted to the Shih Tzu's image as a lap dog. In fact,
his dog is just as hardy and robust as a working
log, as its longevity indicates. It makes an amiable
nd playful companion and is fond of children, but
s also a vigilant watchdog.
)rawbacks: Taking care of the coat is extremely
ime-consuming. It also sheds and carries dirt into
he house. After a walk in bad weather it needs a
pecial cleaning. Tends to yap.
.ife Expectancy: If well cared for, fifteen years,
often even more.

Some Addresses of Breed Clubs

As an address is almost invariably the home of an officer of the breed club, it is understandable that it can change as elections are held. It is wise to check with the American Kennel Club (AKC) at 51 Madison Avenue, New York, NY 10038 for an update on a club's address.

Sporting Dogs

American Pointer Club
Marjorie Mortorella, Secretary
R.D. 2, 331 D
Old Bridge, NJ 08857

German Shorthaired Pointer Club of America, Inc.
Mrs. Marjorie Schulte
P.O. Box 27
Collegeville, PA 19426

German Wirehaired Pointer Club of America
Mr. W. G. Hadlock, Secretary
704 Three Oaks Road
Cary, IL 60013

American Chesapeake Club, Inc.
Ted Holmes, Secretary-Treasurer
A237 N6611 Orchard Drive
Sussex, WI 53089

Flat-Coated Retriever Society of America
Sharon Meyers, Secretary
1011 Woodbine
Northbrook, IL 60062

Golden Retriever Club of America
N. J. Hammand, Secretary
1434 Lincoln
Pomona, CA 91767

Labrador Retriever Club, Inc.
W. K. Laughlin
P.O. Box 1392
Southampton, NY 11968

English Setter Association of America
Mrs. D. J. Roynak, Secretary
11469 Aquilla Road
Chardon, OH 44024

Gordon Setter Club of America
Nancy Zak, Secretary
1 North 521 Prince Crossing
West Chicago, IL 60185

Irish Setter Club of America
Mrs. Geraldine Cuthbert
761 Washington Street
West Melbourne, FL 32901

American Brittany Club
Mrs. LaReine Pittman, Secretary
4124 Birchman
Fort Worth, TX 76107

Clumber Spaniel Club of America
Mrs. Mary Costello
P.O. Box 1455
South Glens Falls, NY 12801

American Spaniel Club
Mrs. M. W. Ciezkowski
12 Wood Lane, Woodsburgh
Woodmere, NY 11598

English Cocker Spaniel Club of America
Mrs. Kate Romanski
P.O. Box 223
Lake Pleasant, MA 01347

Some Addresses of Breed Clubs

English Springer Spaniel Field Trial Association, Inc.
James M. Stewart, Secretary
701 West Butler Pike
Ambler, PA 19002

Irish Water Spaniel Club of America
Helen Keyser, Secretary
9440 Edmundson Drive, Southwest
Salem, OR 97301

Welsh Springer Spaniel Club of America
D. Lawrence Carswell, President
Old Sunrise Highway
Amityville, NY 11701

Vizsla Club of America
May Carpenter, Secretary
P.O. Box 2461
Carmel, CA 93921

Weimaraner Club of America
Jack Alger, Executive Secretary
P.O. Box 6086
Heatherdowns Station
Toledo, OH 43614

Hounds

Afghan Hound Club of America
Mrs. Earl M. Stites
3507 Hallow Creek Road
Arlington, TX 76016

Basenji Club of America
Mrs. Lucretia Hewes
15675 Kata Drive
Elm Grove, WI 63122

Basset Hound Club of America
Mrs. Jean Sheehy
Norwalk-Danbury Road
Georgetown, CT 06829

National Beagle Club
John W. Oelsner, Secretary
8 Baldwin Place
Westpoint, CT 06880

American Bloodhound Club
Ruth G. Anderson, Secretary
4N 730 Brookside West
St. Charles, IL 60174

Borzoi Club of America
Carol Miska, President
904 Main Street
Pittsburgh, PA 15215

Dachshund Club of America, Inc.
Mrs. William Burr Hill
2031 Lake Shore Boulevard
Jacksonville, FL 32210

American Foxhound Club
Jean Dupont McConnell, Secretary
10 Delaware Trust Building
Wilmington, DE 19801

Greyhound Club of America
Dr. Elsie S. Neustadt
P.O. Box 1185
Hanover, MA 02339

Ibizan Hound Club
Dean Wright, President
R.D. 1, Pine Grove Road
Hanover, PA 17331

Some Addresses of Breed Clubs

Irish Wolfhound Club of America
Mrs. William E. Foster, Secretary
R.R. 2 Dean Road
Vermilion, OH 44089

Norwegian Elkhound Association of America
Pat Viken, Secretary
10332 McNerney
Franklin Park, IL 60131

Otter Hound Club of America
Thomas A. St. John, III, Secretary
105 E. 16th Street
New York, NY 10003

Rhodesian Ridgeback Club of America
Sandra Fikes, Secretary
Route 5, Box 78-GL
Mobile, AL 36609

Saluki Club of America
Charlene Kuhl, Secretary
R.D. 1, Box 12
Neshanic, NJ 08853

Scottish Deerhound Club of America
Mrs. Robert F. Hawkins, President
725 West Broadway
Maumee, OH 43537

American Whippet Club
Carol Willumsen, Secretary
124 Vanderbilt Boulevard
Oakdale, NY 11769

Working Dogs

Akita Club of America
Marie Roy, Secretary
43 Vine Street
East Province, RI 02914

Alaskan Malamute Club of America, Inc.
Anne Sholar, Corresponding Secretary
1691 Crest Drive
Encinitis, CA 92024

Bearded Collie Club of America
Mrs. Helen S. Taylor, Secretary
R.F.D. 2, Box 101
Thompson Hill Road
Portland, CT 06480

Belgian Sheepdog Club of America
Gloria L. Davis, Secretary
16 Plateau Road
Baltimore, MD 21221

American Belgian Tervuren Club
Pat Tayler, Secretary
101 Lake Drive
San Bruno, CA 94066

Bernese Mountain Dog Club of America
Gale Werth, Secretary
2976 CTH MM, Route 3
Madison, WI 53711

American Bouvier des Flandres Club
Mrs. Honey Devins, Secretary
R.D. 2, Box 277-2
West Valley Brook Road
Califon, NJ 07830

Some Addresses of Breed Clubs

American Boxer Club, Inc.
Mrs. Lorraine C. Meyer
807 Fairview Boulevard
Rockford, IL 61107

Briard Club of America
Mrs. John A. McLeroth
3030 Rockwood Drive
Fort Wayne, IN 46805

American Bullmastiff Association, Inc.
Tami Raider, Secretary
Nabby Hill
Mohegan Lake, NY 10547

Collie Club of America, Inc.
John Honig
72 Flagg Street
Worcester, MA 01602

Doberman Pinscher Club of America
May S. Jacobson, Corresponding Secretary
32 Clubhouse Lane
Wayland, MA 01778

German Shepherd Club of America
Miss Blanche L. Beisswenger
17 Ivy Lane
Englewood, NJ 07631

Giant Schnauzer Club of America, Inc.
Judy Boston, Secretary
13548 Castelton
Dallas, TX 75234

Great Dane Club of America, Inc.
Mrs. Ernest Riccio, President
89 Hillcrest Road
Hartsdale, NY 10530

Great Pyrenees Club of America
Whitney J. Coombs, Secretary
3119 Valley Road
Millington, NJ 07946

Komondor Club of America
Ms. Nancy Hand, Secretary
159-00 Riverside Drive West
New York, NY 10032

Kuvasz Club of America
Barbara D. Stewart, Secretary
R.F.D. 1
Goffstown, NH 03045

Mastiff Club of America, Inc.
Dr. William R. Newman, Secretary
900 Seton Drive
Cumberland, MD 21502

Newfoundland Club of America
Mrs. William W. Kurth
136 Salem Street
North Andover, MA 01845

Old English Sheepdog Club of America, Inc.
John R. Castor, Secretary
P.O. Box 488
Whitehouse Station, NJ 08889

Puli Club of America, Inc.
Mrs. Dorothea H. Rummel
Pebble Tree Farm
Route 3, Brown Road
Whitewater, WI 53190

Saint Bernard Club of America, Inc.
Joanne Alstede, Secretary
25 Druid Hill Drive
Parsippany, NJ 07054

Some Addresses of Breed Clubs

Samoyed Club of America
Patricia M. McNab, Publicity Officer
8939 Hillview Road
Morrison, CO 80465

America Shetland Sheepdog Association
Rose Tomlin, Corresponding Secretary
107 Cliff Avenue
Pelham, NY 10803

Siberian Husky Club of America
Mrs. Jean Fournier
147 Great Pond Road
Simsbury, CT 06070

Standard Schnauzer Club of America
Barbara Hendrix, Secretary
105 Sheffield Road
Cincinnati, OH 45240

Cardigan Welsh Corgi Club of America, Inc.
Mrs. Doris J. Slaboda
Route 537, Box 97-H
Cream Ridge, NJ 08514

Pembroke Welsh Corgi Club of America
Mrs. Wallace H. Harper, Jr.
Black Brook Road
R.R. 2, Box 170
Pound Ridge, NY 10576

Terriers

Airedale Terrier Club of America
Alma M. Dooley, Secretary
1700 Ogden Avenue
Lisle, IL 60532

Staffordshire Terrier Club of America
Ralph Davis, Secretary
4408 Stanhope
Dallas, TX 75225

Australian Terrier Club of America
Mrs. Milton Fox
1411 Dorsett Dock Road
Point Pleasant, NJ 08742

Bedlington Terrier Club of America
Robert C. Bull, Secretary
P.O. Box 11
Morrison, IL 61270

Border Terrier Club of America
Miss Marjory L. Van der Veer
R.R. 1, Box 276
North Windham, CT 06256

Bull Terrier Club of America
Jill Johnson, Secretary
P.O Box 251, John Street
Lawrence, NY 11559

Cairn Terrier Club of America
Mark W. Alison, Secretary
P.O. Box 462 West Cuba Road
Barrington, IL 60010

Dandie Dinmont Terrier Club of America
Dr. M. Josephine Deubler
2811 Hopkinson House
Washington Square South
Philadelphia, PA 19106

American Fox Terrier Club
Mrs. James A. Farrell, Secretary
P.O. Box 1111
Darien, CT 06820

Some Addresses of Breed Clubs

Irish Terrier Club of America
Robert C. Peters, Secretary
Route Box 103
Dry Fork, VA 24549

United States Kerry Blue Terrier Club
LTC Frances M. Reynolds, Retired
11018 N.E. Davis Street
Portland, OR 97220

United States Lakeland Terrier Club
Robert Komenda, Secretary
91 James Avenue
Atherton, CA 94025

American Manchester Terrier Club
Muriel Henkel, Secretary-Treasurer
4961 Northeast 193 Street
Seattle, WA 98155

American Miniature Schnauzer Club
Mrs. Diana M. Kangas
26 Academy Street
Albion, PA 16401

Norwich and Norfolk Terrier Club
Mrs. Robert B. Congdon, Secretary
15 Morris Street
Merchantville, NJ 08109

Scottish Terrier Club of America
Catherine Ridgley, Corresponding Secretary
801 Leo Street
Dayton, OH 45404

American Sealyham Terrier Club
John S. Stabczyk, Secretary
730 Osborn Road
Naugatuck, CT 06770

Skye Terrier Club of America
Mrs. Robert Boucher
14890 Ostrum Trail North
Marine on Saint Croix, MN 55047

Soft-Coated Wheaten Terrier Club of America
Frank P. Maselli, Jr., Secretary
28 Wright Place
Wilbraham, MA 01095

Welsh Terrier Club of America
Mrs. Neil Benton Hudson
8700 Wolftrap Road
Vienna, VA 22180

West Highland White Terrier Club of America
Mrs. J. W. Williams, Jr., Secretary
2524 Kirby Lane
Jeffersontown, KY 40299

Toys

American Brussels Griffon Association
Mrs. E. N. Hellerman, Secretary-Treasurer
R.D. 1, Old Oak Road
Severn, MD 21144

Chihuahua Club of America
Sandra Cook, Secretary
5680 Morning Creek Circle
College Park, GA 30349

English Toy Spaniel Club of America
Thomas C. Conway
917 Webster Avenue
Anaheim, CA 92804

Some Addresses of Breed Clubs

Italian Greyhound Club of America, Inc.
Lillian Barber, Corresponding Secretary
P.O. Box 743
Morongo Valley, CA 92256

Japanese Chin Club of America
John Milton, Secretary
244 Kavanaugh Way
Pacifica, CA 94044

American Maltese Association
Ann Kannee, Secretary
13209 Banbury Place
Silver Spring, MD 20904

Miniature Pinscher Club of America
Mrs. Lorraine R. Pellinger
3900 Holloway Road
Pineville, LA 71360

Papillon Club of America
Miss Mary Jo Loye
5707 Hillcrest
Detroit, MI 48236

Pekingese Club of America
Iris De La Torre Bueno, Secretary-Treasurer
400 Pelham Road
New Rochelle, NY 10805

American Pomeranian Club
Anthony Piazza, Secretary
125 Stonecliff Drive
Rochester, NY 14614

(Toy) Poodle Club of America, Inc.
Mrs. Stuart Johnson
5330 Ursula Lane
Dallas, TX 75229

Pug Dog Club of America
Mrs. Marjorie D. May
10123 52nd Avenue
College Park, MD 27040

American Shih Tzu Club, Inc.
Donna Steapp, Secretary
P.O. Box 885
Bellaire, TX 77401

Silky Terrier Club of America
Betty Britt, Secretary
P.O. Box 3521
San Francisco, CA 94119

Yorkshire Terrier Club of America, Inc.
Betty Dullinger, Secretary
R.F.D. 2, Box 104
Kezar Falls, ME 04047

Nonsporting Dogs

Bichon Frise Club of America
Bernice Richardson, Secretary
Route 1, Box 292
Kimberly, ID 83341

Boston Terrier Club of America, Inc.
Joan M. Eckert
Cape Road, Box 327
Mendon, MA 01756

Bulldog Club of America
Maryanne Remington, Secretary
4234 Oak Drive Lane
Minnetonka, MI 55343

Some Addresses of Breed Clubs

Chow Chow Club Inc.
Mrs. William Atkinson, Secretary
121 Mountain Drive
South Windsor, CT 06074

Dalmatian Club of America, Inc.
P. Jay Fetner, Secretary
Coachman Farms
Ottsville, PA 18942

French Bulldog Club of America
Mrs. Richard M. Hover
130 Troy Road
Parsippany, NJ 07054

Keeshond Club of America
Mrs. Elmer H. White
Route 1, Box 108
Gunter, TX 75058

American Lhasa Apso Club, Inc.
Janet Whitman
23 Great Oaks Drive
Spring Valley, NY 10972

Poodle Club of America, Inc.
Mrs. Stuart Johnson
5330 Ursula Lane
Dallas, TX 75229

Schipperke Club of America, Inc.
Barbara J. Holl, Secretary
1291 Joliet Street
Dyer, IN 46311

Tibetan Terrier Club of America
Mrs. Alice Smith, Secretary
4 Leslie Road
Ipswich, MA 01938

Index

The numbers printed in *italics* refer to color photos.

Index

Index

Index